Dictionary of genetics, including terms used in cytology, animal breeding and evolution - Primary Source Edition

Knight, Robert L., 1907-

PREFACE

Because genetics is a young science, its workers still often have to coin their own technical terms. This dictionary is an attempt to define and standardise these terms. The first edition will doubtless contain errors and I would be grateful to readers for suggestions as to additions or corrections.

The dictionary is not limited solely to modern terms because students still read, and need to understand, the older books. Also, it is hoped that the inclusion of both older and modern terms will help the coiners of new words to avoid putting an entirely new meaning on an old established word. Moreover, the provision of a full glossary of genetic and allied terms may have the altogether desirable effect of preventing authors from continuing the present trend towards complication of vocabulary. Genetic literature would be more readily understood if writers had, where possible, used an existing term instead of coining a new one. This would have avoided the use for one and the same thing of centromere, kinetochore, kinomere, kinetic constriction, primary constriction, centric constriction, spindle attachment, insertion region, attachment region and attachment constriction. There is much to be said in favor of simplification, and even if simplification of the present vocabulary of genetics is not immediately possible,

Published MCMXLVIII

By the Chronica Botanica Company

of Waltham, Mass., U. S. A.

COPYRIGHT, 1948, by R L KNIGHT

Authorized Agents —

New York, N Y.: STECHERT-HAFNER, INC.
31 East 10th Street

San Francisco, Cal · J W STACEY, INC
551 Market Street

Ottawa, Ont · THORBURN AND ABBOTT, LTD,
104, Sparks Street.

Mexico, D. F : AXEL MORIEL SUCRS,
San Juan de Letran 24-116, Ap. 2762

Lima· LIBRERIA INTERNACIONAL DEL PERU,
Casa Matriz Boza 879, Casilla 1417

Santiago de Chile· LIBRERIA ZAMORANO Y CAPERAN,
Compañia 1015 y 1019, Casilla 362

Rio de Janeiro LIVRARIA KOSMOS,
Rua do Rosario, 135-137, Caixa Postal 3481.

Sao Paulo LIVRARIA CIVILIZACAO BRASILFIRA,
Rua 15 de Novembro, 144

Buenos Aires· ACME AGENCY, SOC DF RESP LTDA,
Casilla de Correo 1136, Suipacha 58

London, W C 2: WM DAWSON AND SONS, LTD,
Chief Agents for the British Empire
Cannon House, Macklin Street.

London, W C 1· H K LEWIS AND CO, LTD,
136, Gower Street

Uppsala: A -B. LUNDEQUISTSKA BOKHANDELN

Groningen: N V ERVEN P. NOORDHOFF.
Chief Agents for Continental Europe

Paris, VI: LIBRAIRIE H LE SOUDIER,
174, Blvd St Germain

Torino· ROSENBERG & SELLIER,
Via Andrea Doria 14

Lisbon LIVRARIA SA DA COSTA,
100-102, R Garrett

Moscow· MEZHDUNARODNAJA KNIGA,
Kuznetski Most 18.

Calcutta, Bombay, and Madras MACMILLAN AND CO, LTD.

Johannesburg: CENTRAL NEWS AGENCY, LTD,
Commissioner & Rissik Sts, P. O Box 1033.

Sydney: ANGUS AND ROBERTSON, LTD.,
89 Castlereagh Street; Box 1516D D G P O

Melbourne, C. 1· N H. SEWARD, PTY, LTD,
457, Bourke Street

*Made and printed in the U S A.
First Printing — First Edition*

OF

GENETICS

Including Terms used in Cytology,
Animal Breeding and Evolution

compiled by

R. L. KNIGHT,

D.Sc., Ph.D., A.I.C.T.A.

Senior Economic Geneticist, Empire Cotton
Growing Corporation and Sudan Government

1948

WALTHAM, MASS., U. S. A.

Published by the Chronica Botanica Company

LOTSYA — A Biological Miscellany

Edited by Frans Verdoorn — Volume 2

Dr J.P. Lotsy

DICTIONARY

of

GENETICS

Born in 1907 in England, the author graduated in Agriculture from Wye College (University of London) in 1927   After two post-graduate years spent at St John's College, Cambridge, and the Imperial College of Tropical Agriculture, Trinidad on a studentship grant from the Empire Cotton Growing Corporation, he was employed as Assistant Plant Breeder under the Corporation and sent on secondment to the Sudan Government, in 1929. In 1937 he was granted an M Sc in Agriculture by the University of London and in 1942 he took the Ph D and in 1947 the D Sc in the same University He now holds the post of Senior Economic Geneticist to the Empire Cotton Growing Corporation and to the Sudan Government

at the least it is to be hoped that writers will not continue to coin new words where suitable recognised terms already exist.

In compiling the dictionary, use has been made of the books and scientific papers listed in the bibliography.

I wish to make grateful acknowledgement to Dr. C. D. DARLINGTON, F.R.S., and to Messrs. J. & A. Churchill Ltd., for permission to reprint a number of definitions from their book "Recent Advances in Cytology"; I am also indebted to the Macmillan Co. of New York for permission to reprint a number of definitions from "The Cell in Development and Heredity" by E. B. WILSON. In addition, a few definitions have been taken direct from "An Ecological Glossary" by J. R. CARPENTER (published by Messrs. Kegan Paul, Trench, Trubner & Co. Ltd.), "A Dictionary of Scientific Terms" by J. F. & W. D. HENDERSON (published by Messrs. Oliver & Boyd Ltd.), "The Chromosomes" by M. J. D. WHITE (published by Messrs. Methuen & Co. Ltd.), "Animal Breeding" by L. M. WINTERS (published by Messrs. John Wiley & Sons, Inc.) and from Volume 28 part 2 of the "Journal of Heredity", and I am grateful to the authors and publishers concerned for permission to do this.

I am indebted to Prof. R. A. FISHER, also to Messrs. Oliver & Boyd Ltd. of Edinburgh, for permission to reprint in abridged form (in Appendix 4), Table No. IV from their book "Statistical Tables for Biological, Agricultural and Medical Research." I am also grateful to Mr. A. J. BATE-MAN, and to the Editors of Nature for permission to reproduce in Appendix 9, a table from "Genetical Aspects of Seed Growing" which appeared in Nature Vol. 157, p. 752.

Finally I am deeply indebted to my wife for her constant help in checking the numerous typescripts which marked the gradual evolution of this book.

R. L. KNIGHT

CONTENTS

Well know I that this lofty lore
  Can scarce in line be pictured true,
Where thoughts abstruse need words unsung before
  So weak our speech is, and the theme so new   .
                                        LUCRETIUS

Å. — Ångström, 0.0000001 mm.

AI, AII. — The first and second anaphases, respectively, in meiosis.

Aberration. — An irregularity in chromosome distribution during heterotypic or homotypic cell division (WINTERS).

Abiogenesis. — Spontaneous generation of living organisms from non-living matter.

Abiogeny. — Abiogenesis, *q.v.*

Abortion. — A miscarriage; arrested development of an organ.

Acarpous. — Devoid of fruit.

Acceleration. — The speeding-up of the time of action of a gene so that the character it controls develops earlier in the life cycle than it did in ancestral forms.

Accessory Chromosomes. — Sex chromosomes, *q.v. See,* also, under W-, X- and Y-chromosomes.

Accidental Evolution. — Evolution which confers no selective advantage and which owes its origin to mutations of more or less neutral effect.

Acclimation. — Adaptation to climatic change on the part of the individual. The physiological adjustment or increased tolerance shown by an individual organism to a change in the surrounding environment. *See* Acclimatization (CARPENTER).

Acclimatization. — The adjustment or increase in tolerance shown by a species in the course of several generations in a changed environment. *See* Acclimation (CARPENTER).

Acentric. — Lacking a centromere.

Acentric-dicentric Translocation. — Aneucentric translocation, *q.v.*

Acentric Inversion. — An inversion of a segment of a chromosome which does not involve the centromere. *cf.* Paracentric Inversion.

Achievement Quotient. — The "educational age" divided by the "mental age". (The child is assigned to an "educational age" on the basis of tests made on subjects taught in school; for "mental age" *see* under Intelligence Quotient).

Achlamydeous. — Possessing neither calyx nor corolla.

Achromasie. — The expulsion of chromatin from a nucleus.

Achromatic Figure. — The frame-work of 'fibres', or striations, which is formed between the two poles and the equatorial region, or between the two centrioles and the equatorial region, during cell division.

Achromatin. — The non-staining basic substance of the nucleus excluding the chromatin

Achromatoplasm. — The non-staining protoplasmic reticulate cell-matrix.

Achrosome. — The structure forming the apex of a mature spermatozoon *cf.* Acroblast

Acidophil. — Having the property of staining heavily in the presence of acid dyes.

Acquired Character. — A structural or functional modification which is impressed on the organism in the course of individual life, but which is not the result of the action of hereditary factors.

Acroblast. — A body, or group of bodies, in the spermatid, derived from the substance of the idiozome and Golgi-bodies, from which arises the acrosome. Variously called 'Idiosome', 'sphere', 'archoplasm', etc (KING; WILSON).

Acrosome. — Achrosome, *q.v.*

Activity-range. — The area within which individuals of a single generation may move.

Adaptation. — (i) Any structural or physiological change on the part of the individual, species, etc., which makes it more fitted to survive under given environmental conditions. (ii) The process of changing in this way.

Adaptive Radiation. — (i) The evolution of several closely related but morphologically and ecologically divergent forms (Cain, 1944). (ii) The presence, within a systematic group, of various types modified to suit mutually exclusive ways of living.

Additive Factors. — Cumulative factors; non-allelomorphic factors affecting the same character and enhancing each other's effect. Such factors are said to show **Additive Effect.**

Adermin. — Vitamin B_6.

Adrenosterone. — An androgenic substance first extracted by Reichstein from the suprarenal cortex.

Afterbirth. — The placenta and foetal membranes when expelled from the uterus following parturition, decidua.

Agamete. — An undifferentiated cell used for reproductive purposes, as opposed to a sexually differentiated reproductive cell or gamete.

Agameon. — A species consisting of only apomictic individuals (CAMP & GILLY).

Agamic, Agamous. — Having no pistils, stamens nor true seeds; reproducing asexually by apomixis, *q.v.*

Agamobium. — The asexual generation of an organism having an alternation of generations.

Agamogenesis. — Asexual reproduction by buds.

Agamogony. — Reproduction by means of undifferentiated cells (agametes), as occurs in *Protista* and *Thallophyta*, as opposed to reproduction by means of sexually differentiated cells (gametes).

Agamospecies. — Species which lack true sexual reproduction.

Agamospermy. — Seed production without fertilization.

"Age and Area". — WILLIS's hypothesis that, other things being equal, species which have existed longest will occur throughout a greater area than species of more recent origin. Thus the localized distribution of an endemic species is explained on the basis of its not having had time to spread, rather than on the theory that it arose as an adaptation brought about by peculiar local conditions.

Agnation. — Relationship through the male line.

Agonisis. — Certation; competition, as between pollen grains of different genotype, in the rapidity with which they can grow down the style.

Agro-ecotype. — A group of agrotypes all having similar environmental preferences.

Agrotype. — An agricultural race.

Akaryote. — A cell lacking a nucleus.

Akinete. — A resting cell.

Albinism. — The absence of chlorophyll in a plant, or of pigmentation in an animal.

Albino. — An animal lacking pigmentation or a plant lacking chlorophyll.

Albinotic. — Affected with albinism.

Alecithal. — Of eggs: having little or no yolk.

Aleurone. — The peripheral thick walled cells of the endosperm of a seed particularly in *Gramineae*.

Allaesthetic Characters. — Characters which become effective via the sense organs and brain of other organisms (HUXLEY).

Allantoin. — A substance which stimulates cell growth; it occurs naturally in the allantoic fluid of mammals, in the urine of sucking calves, etc. and in comfrey roots and it can readily be synthesised. *cf.* Traumatin

Allautogamia. — The state of having a facultative method of pollination in addition to a normal method

Allele. — An allelomorph, *q v.*

Allelic — Allelomorphic (*see* Allelelomorph).

Allelism. — Allelomorphism, *q.v*

Allelomorph — (i) One of a pair of characters which are alternative to each other in inheritance being governed by genes situated at the same locus in homologous chromosomes. (ii) One of a pair, or series, of genes which are alternative to each other in inheritance because they are situated at the same locus in homologous chromosomes Adj. **Allelomorphic.**

Allelomorphism. — A relationship between two factors such that they are of necessity separated into sister gametes in germ cell formation (*see* Allelomorph)

Allen's Rule. — In warm-blooded species, the relative size of exposed portions of the body (limbs, tail and ears) decreases with decrease of mean temperature (HUXLEY)

Allesthetic Characters. — Allaesthetic characters, *q v*

Allocarpy. — The production of fruit following cross-fertilization.

Allochronic Species. — Species which do not belong to the same time level, as opposed to contemporary, or synchronic, species (*cf.* MAYR, 1942).

Allochthonous. — Acquired, extraneous, exotic Opp Autochthonous.

Allogamous. — Reproducing by cross-fertilization.

Allogamy. — Cross-fertilization. Opp Autogamy

Allogene. — PEARSON's term for a recessive allele, as opposed to protogene.

Allogenous Flora. — Relic plants of an earlier prevailing flora and environment, epibiotic plants (CAIN, 1944)

Alloheteroploid. — A heteroploid resulting from the combination of specifically distinct genoms, or chromosomes from such genoms. *cf.* Autoheteroploid.

Alloiobiogenesis — An alternation of a sexual with an asexual form, or, cytologically, the alternation of a haploid with a diploid stage; alternation of generations

Alloiogenesis. — Alloiobiogenesis, *q.v.*

Allometry. — The relation between the growth-rate of a part of an individual and the growth-rate of the whole or of another part; the relationship between growth-rates of different groups, races, genera, etc.

Allomorphosis. — The relation of parts of organisms at some definite age to wholes or parts also at some definite age but of different groups (races, varieties, species, genera) e g egg size or hatching weight to adult size or weight (HUXLEY, NEEDHAM, & LERNER).

Allopatric. — Inhabiting distinct separate areas

Allopatric Hybridization. — Hybridization between incompletely differentiated species, in a border zone, owing to the premature breakdown of a geographic barrier. cf. Sympatric Hybridization.

Alloplasm. — Highly differentiated protoplasm.

Alloploidion. — A species derived by allopolyploidy; its individuals, although usually highly variable, are interfertile (CAMP & GILLY).

Allopolyploid. — An organism with more than two sets of chromosomes in its body cells, derived from two or more species (extant or extinct), by hybridization. cf. Autopolyploid

Allosomal Inheritance. — The inheritance of characters governed by genes located in an allosome, q v

Allosome. — Any a-typical chromosome (especially if its behaviour is a-typical), e g a sex chromosome cf Autosome

Allosynapsis. — Allosyndesis, q v.

Allosyndesis. — Of polyploids the association, in pairs, of homologous chromosomes derived from different parents. cf. Autosyndesis.

Allotetraploid. — An amphidiploid, q.v.

Allotriploid. — An organism having three sets of chromosomes in the body cells, one set being distinct from the other two

Allotropous Flower. — A flower so shaped that its nectar is easy of access to insects.

Allozygote. — PEARSON's term for an organism homozygous for a particular recessive gene, as opposed to protozygote, q.v.

Alternate Dominance. — A theory of sex-determination which supposed all individuals to be heterozygous for sex but that the male determiners were dominant in male offspring and the female determiners dominant in female offspring.

Alternation of Generations. — An alternation of a sexual with an asexual form, or, cytologically, the alternation of a haploid with a diploid stage.

Alternative Inheritance. — Allelomorphism; a relationship between two or more factors such that they are of necessity separated into sister gametes in germ-cell formation; the alternative relationship shown by characters governed by such allelomorphic factors.

Altmann's Granules. — Mitochondria, *q.v.*

Ambisporangiate. — Hermaphrodite (flowers).

Ameiosis. — The replacement of normal meiosis by a single nuclear division so that the chromosome number is not halved.

Ament. — A unisexual, generally bracteate, spike of flowers; a catkin.

Amitosis. — The division of a nucleus by cleavage without separation of daughter chromosomes, so that the latter are not necessarily equally distributed between the daughter nuclei.

Amixia. — Cross-sterility.

Amixis. — The absence of any fertilization process by reason of the absence of sexual differentiation.

Amnion. — One of the fœtal membranes.

Amniotic Cavity. — The space between the fœtus and the amniotic membrane, which is typically filled with the amniotic fluid

Amniotic Sac. — The embryo-sac, female gametophyte or megaspore

Amphiapomict. — An organism which normally reproduces both sexually and apomictically

Amphiaster. — The spindle and its two asters collectively.

Amphibivalent. — An interchange ring of four chromosomes.

Amphiblastic. — Having the bulk of the yolk in one hemisphere, telolecithal.

Amphicarpous. — Producing two kinds of fruit.

Amphidiploid. — The result of hybridization between two plant species or genera where the chromosome set contributed by each parent undergoes doubling and produces in the hybrid a chromosome number which is the sum of the diploid numbers of the two parent forms.

Amphigenesis. — The fusion of gametes to form a zygote.

Amphigony. — Reproduction in which two individuals participate.

Amphikaryon. — A nucleus containing two haploid sets of chromosomes.

Amphimict. — An individual which reproduces by amphimixis.

Amphimictic Population. — A population with free crossing and vital and fertile descendants. Equivalent to panmictic population (CAIN, 1944).

Amphimixis. — The union of maternal and paternal elements in gametic fertilization. Opp. Apomixis.

Amphinucleolus. — A double nucleolus consisting typically of a basophilic and an oxyphilic component in close association (WILSON).

Amphiont. — A zygote; the cell which results from gametic fertilization and, by extension, the individual which grows from this cell.

Amphiplasty. — The loss of a satellite from a chromosome.

Amphitene. — Zygotene; the stage in the prophase of meiosis when homologous chromosomes come together in pairs; the paired chromosome threads at this stage

Amphitoky. — Parthenogenetic multiplication by both sexes.

Amphogenic. — Producing offspring consisting of approximately equal proportions of either sex. N. Amphogeny.

Ampulla of Henle. — An enlargement at the distal end of the vas deferens which acts as a storage place for spermatozoa.

Amyloplasts. — Leucoplasts which take part in the conversion of sugars to starch granules.

Anaboly. — An evolutionary change arising at the end of ontogeny The adding, by a descendant, of a new stage on to the last stage of morphogenesis of the ancestral type· a modified form of overstepping, q.v. "Anaboly differs from 'overstepping' only in that it is the final stage of morphogenesis instead of the definitive adult stage of the ancestor which is passed through in the ontogeny of the descendant" (DE BEER).

Anachromasis. — The changes which take place in a nucleus during prophase.

Anamorphism. — Anamorphosis, q v.

Anamorphosis. — The evolution of one type from another by continuous variation as distinct from evolution brought about by saltation.

Anandrous. — Having no stamens.

Ananthous. — Having no inflorescence.

Anaphase. — The stage in nuclear division when the daughter chromosomes diverge and begin to move towards the poles.

Anaplast, Anaplastid. — Amyloplast, q.v.

Anaschistic. — Bivalents that are said to split "longitudinally" at the first meiotic division; these are bivalents with chiasmata close to the spindle attachment (as opposed to diaschistic) (FARMER & MOORE; DARLINGTON).

Anastomoses. — The fine threads which appear to connect the chromonemata giving a net-like appearance in the resting nucleus.

Androecium. — The stamens collectively

Androgenesis. — Male parthenogenesis; development from a fertilized egg followed by disintegration of the maternal nucleus so that the resulting individual possesses only paternal chromosomes and is typically haploid

Androgenetic. — Of an individual whose cells contain only chromosomes of paternal origin.

Androgenic. — Stimulating the growth or production of male characteristics.

Androgens. — A group of hormonic substances which can induce the development of the secondary sexual characters in a male. The following are included in this group. Testosterone, - propionate, - acetate, - dipropionate, and methyl testosterone.

Androgynary. — Having flowers whose stamens and pistils are petaloid.

Androgyne. — Hermaphrodite

Androgynism. — Bisexuality, hermaphroditism, possessing both stamens and pistils

Androhermaphrodite. — A plant in whose flowers the male organs are developed more strongly than the female; towards the close of the flowering season such a plant may show only male characteristics.

Andromonoecious. — Having both perfect and staminate flowers on the one plant but no pistillate flowers

Andropetalous. — "Double" flowered; with petaloid stamens but pistil unchanged.

Androsomes. — Chromosomes which occur only in nuclei of the male germ-line, never in somatic nuceli of either sex and never in the nuclei of the female germ line, male-limited chromosomes.

Androstenediol. — An androgenic substance which also has oestrogenic effects

Androstenedione. — One of the androgens, said to be more effective than testosterone in maintaining the seminiferous function of the testes.

Androsterone. — A katabolic product of testosterone which is excreted in the urine and which has androgenic properties.

Anemophilous. — Pollinated by wind-borne pollen

Anemophily. — Wind-pollination

Aneucentric Translocation. — A translocation involving the centromere so that an acentric chromosome and a dicentric chromosome result.

Aneuploid. — An organism whose somatic nuclei do not contain an exact multiple of the haploid number of chromosomes, one or more chromosomes being represented more times than the rest; an irregular, or unbalanced, polyploid *cf* Orthoploid.

Aneurin, Aneurine. — Vitamin B_1 ($C_{12}H_{18}N_4SOCl_2$) the anti-neuritic vitamin, thiamine, thiamin.

Ångström. — 0000001 mm.

Anhydro-hydroxy-progesterone. — Pregneninolone, a progesterone-like substance which retains its activity when administered orally

Anisogamete. — A gamete which differs morphologically or in size from its partner, heterogamete

Anisogamy. — (i) Conjugation of anisogametes, heterogamy. (ii) The state of having anisogametes

Anisogenomatic. — Of a chromosome complement composed of two, or more, non-homologous sets.

Anisogenous — Of plants whose male and female gametes behave dissimilarly in the transmission of inherited characters. N. Anisogeny. *cf* Isogenous.

Anisogeny. — *See* Anisogenous.

Anisoploid. — (i) Having an odd number of sets of chromosomes in the somatic cells (ii) An individual of this type.

Anisopolyploidy. — The state of having an odd number of sets of chromosomes in the somatic cells.

Anisotropy. — Of ova. having a predetermined axis.

Anlage. — Foundation or 'scaffolding' of embryo. Primitive elements out of which a cell, organ or organism is formed (BEADNELL)

Anoestrum, Anoestrus. — The resting period, or period of absence of sexual desire which recurs between heat periods in mammals; the period when the female is not 'on heat'.

Anorthospiral. — Having a spiralization of such a type that a secondary compensational twisting occurs in the substance of the thread, in addition to the straight-forward twist of the spiral. *cf.* Orthospiral

Anovular Menstruation. — Periodic uterine bleeding similar to that of menstruation but occurring in the absence of ovulation and, consequently, of any corpus luteum

Anther. — The upper, fertile, part of a stamen, containing the pollen.

Antheridial Mother-cell. — A cell within the pollen grain of flowering plants which divides to form the male gametes (BOWER).

Anthesis. — The bursting of the anthers; the expansion of the flower; the time when fertilization takes place; the period from the bursting of the bud to the setting of the fruit.

Anthropogenesis. — The evolutionary descent of man.

Anticipation. — A tendency for a character to become manifest at an increasingly early age in each successive generation

Anticipation, Law of. — The age of onset of dementia tends to be earlier in each successive generation of the family, until it finally culminates in amentia. (Later work casts considerable doubt on this "Law".)

Anti-haemorrhagic Vitamin. — Vitamin K.

Anti-neuritic Vitamin. — Vitamin B_1.

Anti-nyctalopia Vitamin. — Vitamin A.

Antipodal Cone. — The cone of astral rays opposite the spindle (VAN BENEDEN; WILSON).

Anti-rachitic Vitamin. — Vitamin D.

Anti-recapitulation. — The resemblance of an adult descendent to an ancestral embryo so that the descendent loses from its life-history the adult ancestral characters.

Anti-scorbutic Vitamin. — Vitamin C

Anti-sterility Vitamin. — Vitamin E.

Antithetic Generations. — Alternate generations of haploid and diploid type which are morphologically distinct.

Antithetical Dominance. — *See* Dominance, Hypothesis of Antithetical

Anti-xerophthalmia Vitamin. — Vitamin A.

Apatetic Coloration. — Protective coloration.

Apetalous. — Lacking petals

Aphallism. — The state of having no penis. Adj. **Aphallic.**

Apocarpy. — The condition of having the carpels separate.

Apocyte. — A multinucleate mass of protoplasm arising either by nuclear division or cell fusion *cf.* Coenocyte and Syncytium

Apogameon. — A species containing both apomictic and non-apomictic individuals (CAMP & GILLY)

Apogamogony. — Agamospermy when followed by an alternation of generations.

Apogamous.— *See* Apogamy.

Apogamy. — The production of seed or progeny by sexual organs or related structures without fertilization, the embryos being formed from haploid nuclei (but not from ova). Typically the embryo is formed by the development of two fused embryo-sac cells. (*See* Apomixis). Adj. **Apogamous.** *See* under Reproduction

Apogeny. — Sterility resulting from loss or destruction of sexual organs.

Apogyny. — Female sterility.

Apolegamy. — Selective breeding.

Apomeiosis. — The formation of a gametophyte with an unreduced chromosome number.

Apomict. — An individual (race, species, etc.) which reproduces by apomixis, *q v.*

Apomixis. — Reproduction in which the sexual organs, or related structures, take part, but in which there is no fertilization so that the resulting seed is of vegetative nature (as opposed to amphimixis, *q.v.*) Adj. **Apomictic.** Apomixis includes Parthenogenesis, Apogamy and Apospory, *q.v. See* under Reproduction. Apomixis is used by CAIN (1944) in the sense of the phenomenon of limited or no cross-reproduction — the opposite of panmixy.

Apopetalous. — Without petals; apetalous.

Aporogamy. — Fertilization in which the pollen-tube, in reaching the ovule, does not pass through the micropyle.

Aposematic Coloration. — Warning coloration; distinctive coloration associated with unpalatability or with other unpleasant characteristics tending to make the individual unattractive to a predator

Aposeme. — A group of unpalatable individuals all having closely similar warning coloration (*see* Aposematic Coloration), but not necessarily all of one species.

Apospory. — Development of a gametophyte from an unreduced cell (not the spore-mother-cell) with a somatic chromosome complement. *See* under Reproduction

Apparato Reticolare. — The Golgi Apparatus, *q v.*

Apyrene. — Of spermatozoa: having no nucleus.

A. Q. — Achievement quotient, *q v.*

Arber's Law of Loss. — The general rule that a structure or organ once lost in the course of phylogeny can never be regained (ARBER).

Archallaxis. — An evolutionary change arising in early ontogeny.

Archebiosis. — Source of life, abiogenesis.

Archespore, Archesporium. — The cell or group of cells from which the spores are formed. Adj **Archesporial.**

Archetype. — The primitive type from which later types have evolved.

Archigenesis. — Abiogenesis, *q.v.*

Archigony. — Abiogenesis, *q v.*

Archiplasm. — The protoplasm which makes up the spindle fibres and astral rays. The chromophobic portion of the Golgi apparatus

Archoplasm. —Archiplasm, *q v.*

Armogenesis. — Adaptation on the part of the embryo.

Armogony. — Armogenesis, *q v.*

Aromorphosis. — Large changes of general adaptive significance which do not restrict the possibilities of life of the type (DE BEER).

Arrhenogenic. — Producing offspring consisting entirely, or almost entirely, of males. N. **Arrhenogeny.**

Arrhenoplasm — Male protoplasm, as distinct from female protoplasm or thelyplasm.

Arrhenotoky. — Production of males by parthenogenesis.

Arrhostia. — Any physical condition, arising as a result of evolution, which simulates a diseased state. Adj. **Arrhostic.**

Arrhostic. — *See* Arrhostia.

Artefact, Artifact — Any structure or appearance which is not typical of the actual specimen, but which results from laboratory or other treatment

Artenkreis. — A circle of related species that show a geographical replacement pattern (CAIN, 1944)

Artificial Insemination. — The introduction of spermatozoa into the uterus (or vagina) by mechanical means without coitus taking place.

Artificial Parthenogenesis. — The induction of development of an unfertilized ovum by chemical or physical stimulation.

Aschheim-Zondek Test. — A pregnancy test based on the stimulation of the development of the ovaries of an immature mouse following injection into the mouse of urine from a pregnant woman.

Ascorbic Acid. — Vitamin C; hexuronic acid, $C_6H_8O_6$; a water-soluble, anti-scorbutic vitamin

Asexual.— Lacking functional sexual organs, sexless, without sex

Aspermia — The state of being devoid of semen

Assortative Mating. — A tendency for like to mate with like.

Assortive Mating. — Assortative Mating, *q v.*

Assortment. — The separation of genes, or of chromosomes, of maternal and paternal origin at meiosis.

Aster. — (i) The radial, star-like, protoplasmic striations which surround the centrosome during cell division. (ii) Used at one time to denote any star-like group of chromosomes at mitosis

Astrocentre. — The centrosome; the self propagating activity-centre in cell division in most animal cells and in the **Thallophyta.**

Astrosphere. — A collective term for the centrosome together with the surrounding aster zone; centrosphere; attraction sphere.

Asynapsis. — Asyndesis, *q.v.*

Asynaptic. — Asyndetic. *See* Asyndesis.

Asyndesis. — Absence of the fusion of homologous chromosomes during meiosis Adj **Asyndetic**

Asyndetic. — *See* Asyndesis

Asyngamic. — Unable to cross by reason of differences in time of flowering.

Atavism. — The reappearance of a character after a lapse of one or more generations, due to the character being recessive or being dependent on complementary factors, or as a result of back-mutation Atavism is sometimes called "throwing back" (to an ancestor) and the aberrant individual is termed a "throw-back".

Atelomitic. — Applied to chromosomes with non-terminal spindle attachments.

Attached X-chromosomes. — X-chromosomes which are attached to each other at their centromere ends.

Attachment Chromomere. — The attachment particle or centrogene as distinct from the attachment region or centromere.

Attachment Constriction. — Centromere; spindle attachment; insertion region; kinetochore; a non-staining localized region in each chromosome which remains single for some time after the rest of the chromosome has divided and which appears to be 'attached' to the spindle 'fibre'

Attachment Region. — Attachment Constriction *q.v*

Attraction Particle. — A central granule in the centrosome; centriole.

Attraction Sphere. — Astrosphere; centrosphere; a collective term for the centrosome together with the surrounding aster zone.

Attraction Spindle. — The terminal portions of the spindle.

Auto-alloploid. — An organism which has originated by a doubling of the chromosome complement of an allotetraploid.

Autoauxone. —— Any substance which is biologically highly active and which is synthesized by the organism itself.

Autocarp. — A fruit obtained as the result of self-fertilization.

Autocarpy. — Fruiting following self-fertilization. Adj. **Autocarpic.**

Autochthonous. — (i) Indigenous. (ii) Innate, hereditary, inherited. Opp. Allochthonous.

Autogamous. — Reproducing by self-fertilization.

Autogamy. — (1) Fertilization by self pollination. (ii) Union of closely related cells.

Autogenesis. — Spontaneous generation of living matter from non-living matter, autogeny, autogony, abiogenesis.

Autogeny, Autogony. — Autogenesis, *q.v.*

Autogenous Variations. —— Heritable variations (as opposed to variations due to environment), *e.g.* recombinations, gene mutations, chromosome changes.

Autogony. — Autogeny, Autogenesis, *q.v.*

Autoheteroploid. — A heteroploid resulting from multiplication of a single genom or of certain chromosomes from a single genom. *cf* Alloheteroploid.

Autoicous. — Having staminate and pistillate flowers on the one plant.

Automixis. — The fusion of two nuclei derived from a common mother-cell.

Auto-orientation. — *See* under Orientation.

Autoparthenogenesis. — The development of an unfertilized egg as a result of artificial stimulation by chemical, or other, means

Autophilous. — Autogamous; self-pollinated.

Autopolyploid. — An organism having more than two homologous sets of chromosomes in its body cells, derived from a single parent species; duplicational polyploid; autotetraploid *cf* Allopolyploid.

Autosexing. — Used of strains the two sexes of which are readily recognizable by reason of the presence of a sex-linked gene, *e.g.* barring in chickens

Autosomes. — Normal chromosomes (as opposed to sex chromosomes); euchromosomes. *cf.* Allosome.

Autosynapsis. — Autosyndesis, *q.v.*

Autosyndesis. — The pairing, in a polyploid or allopolyploid, of chromosomes (i) derived from the same parental gamete, or (ii) phylogenetically derived from the same diploid species.

Autotetraploid. — A tetraploid whose nuclei contain four sets of chromosomes of the same origin; duplicational polyploid.

Autotriploid. — An individual having three homologous sets of chromosomes in the body cells.

Auxesis. — The chemical or physical induction of cell division.

Auxetic. — Any substance which induces, or increases, cell division.

Auximone. — A growth-stimulating substance in plant food.

Auxin. — $C_{18}H_{32}O_5$, a growth promoting plant hormone produced at growing points

Auxocyte. — A mother-cell whose nucleus has started to divide meiotically.

Auxone. — Any substance which is biologically highly active.

Auxospireme. — The spireme-thread in meiosis which appears after the association of homologous chromosomes at syndesis.

Azygosperm. — A spore formed from an unfertilized gamete; parthenospore; azygospore.

Azygospore. — Azygosperm, *q v.*

Azygote. — An individual produced as a result of haploid parthenogenesis

B$_1$, B$_2$, B$_3$. — First, second and third backcrosses respectively

B-indolylacetic Acid. — A plant growth stimulant present in urine, heteroauxin.

Backcross. — A cross between a hybrid and either of its parents, or between a heterozygote and a homozygous recessive.

Backcross Parent. — That parent of a hybrid with which it is again crossed or with which it is repeatedly crossed; recurrent parent.

Backcross Ratios. — The proportion of heterozygotes to bottom recessives expected in a backcross is given by calculating 2^n where n is the number of factors involved, *e.g.* with 2 factors $2^n = 4$ and the expected ratio is 3.1 with 3 factors $2^n = 8$ and the expected ratio is 7 1, etc.

Background Adaptation — The agreement between the colour and appearance of an organism and the general appearance of the environment in which it lives.

Back-mutation. — The mutation of a mutant gene back to its original state.

Back-Pollinating. — Backcrossing. *See* Backcross.

Baculiform. — Of chromosomes rod-shaped.

Balance. — A state of harmonious adjustment of the interaction of the genes or chromosomes of an organism so that its development is normal Opp Unbalance

Balance, Secondary. — A new balance derived by change in the proportion of genes, as in a secondary polyploid, from an old balance and capable of competing with it (DARLINGTON & MOFFETT)

Balanced Lethals. — Closely linked lethal factors located in chromosomes of opposite gametes so that crossing over is infrequent and the factors remain in repulsion.

Balanced Polymorphism. — *See* under Polymorphism.

Balbiani-type Chromosomes. — Giant chromosomes whether occurring in salivary glands or elsewhere. *cf* Salivary Gland Chromosomes.

Basic Number. — The number of chromosomes found, or assumed to have occurred, in the gametes of a diploid ancestor (extant or extinct) of a polyploid.

Basichromatin. — (i) A deeply staining type of chromatin rich in nucleic acid (ii) Chromatin

Basifixed. — Of anthers. attached to the filaments by their bases.

Basiphilic, Basophilic. — Staining readily with basic dyes.

Bastard Merogony. — *See* under Merogony

Batesian Mimicry. — The resemblance of an innocuous species to another species which is protected from predatory types by unpalatability or by other qualities. *cf.* Mullerian —.

Bathmic Force. — A hypothetical, inherent, adaptive growth-force supposed to bring about variation and to control evolution.

Batonette. — Part of the Golgi Apparatus, *q v*

Bergmann's Rule. — Within a polytypic warm-blooded species, the body-size of a subspecies usually increases with decreasing mean temperature of its habitat (HUXLEY).

Bigener, Bigeneric Cross. — An intergeneric hybrid

Bioblast — A hypothetical, self-propagating, vital unit of granular structure in the cytoplasm.

Biocatalyzer. — Any substance, whether organic or inorganic, which is biologically highly active. The biocatalyzers include such substances as manganese and zinc and also enzymes, ergones, vitamins and hormones

Biogen, Biogene. — *See* under Biophore.

Biogenesis. — The doctrine of life from life, as opposed to "Spontaneous" Generation. Opp. Abiogenesis

Biogenetic Law. — The hypothesis that ontogeny recapitulates phylogeny *See* Recapitulation

Biogeny. — The study of evolution.

Biologic Isolation. — The isolation of one species from its congeners by reason of interspecific sterility, incompatibility, preferential mating or differences in time of sexual activity

Biological Race. — (i) Such a "race may be said to exist where the individuals of a species can be divided into groups usually isolated to some extent by food preferences occurring in the same locality and showing definite differences in biology, but with corresponding structural differences either few or inconstant or completely absent" (THORPE, 1930). (ii) In diseases the term denotes a strain which, though morphologically indistinguishable yet differs from the normal in its pathogenicity.

Biomass. — A general term for any wide group of organisms

Biometry. — The branch of science which deals with the application of statistical methods to biological investigations.

Bion. — A hypothetical element which was thought to be present in living matter, its function being the control of evolution.

Biophore. — WEISMANN postulated that each determinant (gene) is made up of a complex of biophores which he regarded as the smallest ultimate units of living matter. A biophore is the equivalent of the biogen of VERWORN

Bioplasm. — Protoplasm; living cell substance including the nucleus and cytoplasm

Biosystematy. — Taxonomic studies involving cytology and genetics.

Biotin. — A component of the vitamin B_2 complex.

Biotope. — The smallest natural area or space characterized by a particular environment (CAIN, 1944).

Biotype. — A group of individuals all of one genotype.

Biparous. — Giving birth to two offspring at a time.

Birefringent. — Of chromosomes, etc.· having certain types of regular molecular or micellar patterns, usually detectable by the use of polarized light.

Bisexual. — Hermaphrodite, having both male and female reproductive organs in one individual.

Bivalent. — Two chromosomes containing approximately the same gene loci which have come together side-by-side at zygotene and which are held together by chiasmata or by mutual attraction. *See* Univalent and Chromatid.

Blastogenesis. — (i) Germplasm inheritance, the transmission of hereditary characters by the germplasm as distinct from transmission by the cytoplasm. (ii) Reproduction by budding.

Blastogenic. — Of, or pertaining to, the germplasm.

Blastomere. — Any one of the cells formed during the first few divisions of the animal egg

Blastula. — The stage in the development of the zygote during which the embryo-cells are arranged in the form of a hollow sphere.

Bleeder. — A hæmophilic individual.

Blending Characters. — Characters which merge, thus failing to show the clear-cut segregation typical of mendelian heredity. *See* Blending Inheritance

Blending Inheritance. — Inheritance in which clearly defined segregation is lacking in F_2 This is generally due to the presence of multiple factors independently inherited.

Block Mutation. — A term used to denote a change in, or the omission of, a group of adjacent genes (CHITTENDEN).

Blood-line. — Pedigree; relationship; family.

Bottom Recessive. — An individual homozygous for the recessive alleles of all the genes under investigation.

Bouquet Stage. — The zygotene and pachytene stages in organisms in which a polarization of the chromosomes, with their centromeres towards one side of the nucleus, occurs during the prophase of meiosis.

Brachymeiosis. — A modified form of meiosis in which no second division occurs.

Bracteody. — The replacement of the floral whorls by bracts.

Bradyauxesis. — A growth relationship in which the growth of a part of an individual is slower than that of the body as a whole.

Bradytelic. — Evolving considerably slower than the modal rate. *cf.* Horotelic and Tachytelic.

Branched Chromosome. — *See* Chromosomes.

"Breakage First" Hypothesis. — The theory that chromosomes can suffer fragmentation after which the fragments may either remain loose, or become reattached to restore the original gene arrangement, or may unite with other fragments to form new aggregates (*cf.* DOBZHANSKY, 1941).

Breed. — A group of individuals having a common origin and possessing certain distinguishing characteristics not common to other members of the same species (WINTERS).

Breeding. — The science, or art, of improving or changing plants or animals.

Breeding, 'Family' Method of. — In this system each female is mated to a single male and her offspring recorded.

Breeding, Sib Method of. — *See* Breeding, 'Family' Method of.

Brephic. — Pertaining to primitive or larval growth.

Brochonema. — The looped spireme thread in mitosis or meiosis.

Brood. — A number of offspring from a single birth or from a single clutch of eggs.

Brusque Variation. — A sudden, heritable deviation from type; mutation.

Budding. — A form of grafting in which the scion consists of a bud which is inserted under the bark of the stock.

Bud Mutation. — Bud-sport, *q.v.*

Bud-sport. — a somatic mutation or variation arising in a bud and producing an abnormal branch.

Buffering Genes. — A complex of polygenes controlling the expression of a major gene and reducing the variability of its phenotype by toning down its reaction to environmental differences *See* Canalized Development Hypothesis

Bulbil. — A modified bud capable of developing into a new plant when separated from the parent plant.

Bulk Method of Breeding. — The growing of segregating generations of a hybrid of self-pollinated crops in a bulk plot, with or without mass selection, followed by individual plant selection in F_6 or later generations (HAYES & IMMER).

Burdizzo Pincers. — Double-hinged pincers used in emasculation for crushing the spermatic cord.

Burdo. — A graft hybrid which arises as a result of nuclear fusion as between the nuclei of stock and scion.

C_0, C_1, C_2, C_3. — Acentric, monocentric, dicentric and tri-centric Chromatids are distinguished from chromosomes by a single superscript for the former and a double superscript for the latter: C^1, C^{11}.

C_1, C_2, C_3. — The first, second and third 'generations' of vegetative propagation

C-mitosis. — The type of abnormal mitosis, produced by colchicine treatment, in which the spindle is inactivated and the chromosomes become scattered in the cytoplasm where they form the characteristic configurations known as 'c-pairs'

C-pairs — *See* under C-mitosis.

Cacogenesis, Kakogenesis. — (i) Inability to hybridize (HENDERSON). (ii) Deterioration of race or strain

Cacogenic, Kakogenic. —— Dysgenic, tending to impair the qualities of the race, or strain.

Caenogenesis. — The production of a new evolutionary form during ontogeny, especially the appearance of novel embryonic features; youthful adaptation; clandestine evolution.

Caenogenetic. — Of recent origin, of a character which affects only the young stages of ontogeny in a race.

Calciferol. — $C_{28}H_{44}O$, Vitamin D_2

Calycanthemy. — Petalody of the calyx; the formation of coloured petal-like structures in place of a normal calyx

Calyciflorus. — Having calyx, corolla and stamens adnate.

Calyx. — The outermost of the floral whorls.

Canalicular Apparatus. — The Golgi Apparatus, *q.v.*

Canalized Development Hypothesis. — The hypothesis that although an organism may follow any one of a number of developmental paths, it is difficult to make it develop along lines intermediate between these possibilities because the integrated genotype acts as a buffering system, in such a way as to limit the variation of the organism's response to environmental fluctuations (MATHER).

Capitulum. — An inflorescence composed of numerous sessile florets closely arranged on a receptacle *e g Compositae.*

Caponise, Caponising. — Castration of a male bird.

Caprification. — The process of pollinating figs (often by attracting Fig Insects by hanging inedible caprifigs in the trees).

Carotene. — Provitamin A, $C_{40}H_{56}$; a group of three orange coloured pigments found in plants (particularly in th chloroplasts) from which the liver manufactures vitamin A.

Carotin. — Carotene. $q\,v.$

Carpel. — A floral-leaf bearing ovules. In monocarpellary flowers the carpel is the ovary, style and stigma collectively.

Carpoxenia. — Direct effect of the fertilizing pollen upon the maternal tissues of the carpel. $cf.$ Xenia.

Caryotin. — The material comprising the nuclear reticulum including both basichromatin and oxychromatin.

Castration. — Removal, or destruction, of the male gonads or testes.

Catenation. — The formation of rings or chains by chromosomes at diakinesis.

Catkin. — A pendulous uni-sexual spike of flowers; ament

Caul. — The amnion, particularly when this closely envelopes the face of a child at birth.

Cell. — The structural unit of living organisms, consisting basically of nucleus, cytoplasm, and, in plants, a cell wall

Cell Conjugation. — Union or fusion of cells.

Cell Division. — See under Amitosis, Mitosis and Meiosis.

Cell Granule. – Ectosome, $q.v.$

Cell Plate. — The first stage in the formation of a cell wall between daughter cells.

Cell Sap. — The more fluid material of a cell.

Cellulose. — $(C_6H_{10}O_5)_x$. A carbohydrate forming the basic ground substance of cell walls.

Cenobium. — A mass of undifferentiated cells or of unicellular organisms $cf.$ Coenocyte.

Cenogeny, Cenogenetic. — Caenogenesis, Caenogenetic, $q\,v.$

Central Body. — (1) Centrosome, $q\,v.$ (11) The structures at the centre of the aster during mitosis.

Central Spindle. — A miniature spindle which, where centrosomes and asters are present, may form between them, and which, on the disappearance of the nuclear membrane (at prometaphase) moves into the middle of the nuclear zone.

Centric — Possessing a centromere.

Centric Constriction. — Spindle attachment constriction; centromere.

Centriole. — A central deeply staining particle in the centrosome. This in some organisms replaces the centrosome.

Centrodesmose, Centrodesmus, Centrodesm. — The delicate fibril (or fibrils) joining the two centrosomes at mitosis.

Centrogene. — The attachment *particle* as distinct from the attachment *region* or centromere.

Centrolecithal. — Of ova: having the yolk centrally placed.

Centromere. — Spindle attachment; insertion region; kinetochore; a non-staining, localized region in each chromosome to which the spindle 'fibre' appears to be attached at metaphase. The centromere remains single for some time after the rest of the chromosome has divided, and, at anaphase, starts to move towards the pole before the rest of the chromatid

Centronucleus. — A nucleus that contains a central body or which itself plays the part of a division centre (BOVERI: WILSON).

Centroplasm. — The protoplasm in the centrosphere zone during cell division

Centroplast. — An extranuclear spherical body forming division centre of mitosis in certain lower organisms (HENDERSON).

Centrosome. — The self-propagating centre of activity in cell division in most animal cells and in the *Thallophyta* It consists of an attraction sphere which may contain a small highly staining granule (centriole) and it appears to determine the orientation of the spindle

Centrosphere. — The less deeply staining substance which surrounds the centriole and makes up the body of the centrosome. In organisms lacking a centriole the centrosphere is synonymous with the centrosome

Centrosphere, Giant. — According to LEWIS (1920) this consists of a centriole contained within a medullary zone which stains deeper than an external cortical zone and from which it is separated by a thin membrane (LUDFORD, 1945).

Centrotheca. — Idiozome, *q.v.*

Centrum. — Central body, *q.v.*

Cephalization. — Tendency in ascending evolution to specialization of anterior end of organisms (BEADNELL).

Cephalobrachial. — Of a chromosome: bearing a terminal, knob-like extension.

Certation. — Competition as between pollen grains of different genotype, in the rapidity with which they can grow down the style; agonisis.

Cervix (uteri). — The neck of the uterus leading into the vagina

Cevitamic Acid. —— Vitamin C

Character, Characteristic. — The phenotypic result of the interaction of a gene or group of genes and the environment

Character Gradients. — Clines, $q\,v$

Character-unit. — An obsolete synonym for gene

Chasmogamy. — The opening of the perianth at the time of flowering, as opposed to cleistogamy Adj Chasmogamic.

Check Cross — A cross of an individual of unknown genotype with a phenotypically similar individual of known genotype in order to determine, in F_2, whether the same gene or allelic series is responsible for the phenotypic appearance of both individuals.

Chemo-differentiation. — The initial stage of cell differentiation in which cytoplasmic chemical changes occur unaccompanied by any visible change in the cells.

Chi. — *See* Appendix 1

Chiasma-ta. — An exchange of partners in a system of paired chromatids, observed between diplotene and the beginning of the first anaphase in meiosis (JANSSENS, DARLINGTON). A visible change of pairing affecting two out of the four chromatids in a bivalent at meiosis; an outward sign that a genetical cross-over has taken place (WHITE) *See* also under Comparate ——, Complementary ——, Disparate ——, Distal ——, Inversion ——, Proximal ——, Reciprocal ——, Symmetrical ——.

    Compensating ——. Where one chiasma restores the association interrupted by the other (NEWTON & DARLINGTON).

    Imperfect ——. Where one of the four associations in a chiasma is broken prior to anaphase (DARLINGTON)

    Interstitial ——. Where there is a length of chromatid on both sides of the chiasma (DARLINGTON).

    Lateral —— A chiasma which is terminal as to two chromatids and interstitial as to the others. Of two kinds, symmetrical and asymmetrical (DARLINGTON)

    Multiple ——. A terminal chiasma where three or four pairs of chromatids are engaged (DARLINGTON)

    Terminal ——. Those which occur at the extremities of the chromatids.

Chiasma Frequency. — The average number of chiasmata formed per bivalent, or in any particular bivalent, in a given organism under given circumstances.

Chiasma Theory of Pairing. — The hypothesis that whenever two chromosomes which have been paired at pachytene remain associated until metaphase they do so by virtue of the formation of a chiasma or visible exchange of partners amongst their chromatids (DARLINGTON).

Chiasmatype Hypothesis. — The part of the chiasmatype theory which supposes that chiasmata are determined by crossing-over between two dissimilar chromatids of the four involved (DARLINGTON, 1932)

Chiasmatype Theory. — The theory that crossing-over is connected with chiasma formation

Chiasmatypy. — The process of chiasma formation together with its genetical implications

Chimaera — A plant composed of tissues of two, or more, genetically distinct types *See* Burdo, Chromosomal ——, Dichlamidius, Diplochlamydeous ——, Graft Hybrid, Gynandromorph, Haplochlamydeous ——, Hyperchimaera, Mericlinal ——, Mixochimaera, Monochlamydeous ——, Mosaic, Periclinal ——, Polychlamydeous ——, Polyclinal ——, Sectorial ——, Trichlamydeous

Chiropterophilous. — Pollinated by means of bats.

Chloranthy. — The reversion of petals to green leaves

Chlorophyll — Two green chemical compounds, which together enable plants to obtain energy from light for use in the synthesis of substances from carbon dioxide and water. The two components are Chlorophyll a, $C_{55}H_{72}O_5N_4Mg$ and Chlorophyll b, $C_{55}H_{70}O_6N_4Mg$, there are typically associated with two yellow compounds, carotin, $C_{40}H_{56}$, and xanthophyll, $C_{40}H_{56}O_2$.

Chloroplast. — A small dense protoplasmic cell inclusion containing chlorophyll sometimes accompanied by other pigments.

Chlorosis. — A yellowing of the plant due to chlorophyll deficiency, chlorophyll deficiency

Chlorotic. — Lacking chlorophyll.

Choline. — A component of the vitamin B_2 complex

Chondriocont, Chondriokont. — A rod-like or thread-like chondriosome.

Chondriolysis. — Disintegration of mitochondria.

Chondrioma, Chondriome. — The collective term for the mitochondria of any individual cell.

Chondriomere — That part of a spermatozoon in which the chondriosomes occur, plastomere.

Chondriomite. — A linear type of chondriosome having the appearance of a string of granules.

Chondriosomal Mantle. — A mass of chondriosomes around a nucleus at mitosis.

Chondriosomes. — Self-propagating bodies, with low refraction, in the cytoplasm, including mitochondria, Golgi-bodies, chondriospheres, chondrioconts, chondriomites and chondrioplasts. "Mitochondria or chondriosomes are elements of definite form in the cytoplasm of all cells. They lie freely in the cytoplasm, possess the power of independent movement and may take the form of filaments, of rods, or of granules" (BOURNE, 1945).

Chondriosphere. — A spherical chondriosome, made up of several chondriosomes which have coalesced

Choriheterosis. — The stimulus causing heterocaryotic vigour in the fungi (DODGE)

Chorology. — The geographic study of the distribution of organisms.

Chromasie. — The augmentation of chromatin (in a nucleus).

Chromatic Sphere. — A daughter nucleus at telophase in cell division.

Chromatid. — A half chromosome between early prophase and metaphase of mitosis and between diplotene and second metaphase in meiosis — after which stages, *i.e.* during an anaphase, it is known as a daughter chromosome The separating chromosomes at the first anaphase are known as daughter bivalents, or, if single chromatids derived from the division of univalents, daughter univalents (MCCLUNG; DARLINGTON)

Chromatid Break. — A break in one of two sister chromatids which persists as such. Such breaks may be produced by X-ray treatment

Chromatid Bridge. — Chromosome Bridge, *q v.*

Chromatid Interchanges. — These "involve breaks in two (or more) chromatids or in different loci of the same chromatid, and reunion in new ways" (LEA & CATCHESIDE).

Chromatid Non-disjunction. — The passing of homologous parts of chromatids to the same pole following crossing-over between homologous differential segments in a multiple interchange hybrid (E. SANSOME; DARLINGTON).

Chromatid Tie. — The link which exists between two non-crossed-over homologous chromatids through their crossed-over sister chromatids.

Chromatids, Sister. — Those derived from division of one and the same chromosome, as opposed to **non-sister chromatids** which are derived from partner chromosomes at pachytene (DARLINGTON).

Chromatin. — A densely staining substance in the nucleus; the part of the chromosome that stains deeply with basic dyes during mitosis.

Chromatin Bridge. — Chromosome bridge, *q.v.*

Chromatoid Bodies. — Chromophilic structures which occur in the cytoplasm of spermatocytes.

Chromatolysis. — The dissolution of chromatin.

Chromatophore. — Chromoplast; a pigment cell in animals or a pigmented plastid (not necessarily a chloroplast) in plants

Chromatoplasm. — (i) Vegetative protoplasm as distinct from idioplasm. (ii) Pigmented granular protoplasm as opposed to colourless achromatoplasm.

Chromatospherite. — Nucleolus, a darkly staining body occurring in the nuclei of most cells.

Chromidia. — Particles of chromatin in the cytoplasm surrounding the nucleus.

Chromidiogamy. — The union, in gametic fertilization, of the chromidia from the two parents.

Chromidiosomes. — The minute particles of chromatin which make up the chromidia.

Chromiole. — A minute granule (possibly an artefact) forming part of a chromomere.

Chromoblast. — A proto-pigment-cell.

Chromocentre. — (i) An agglomeration of chromatin in the nucleus. (ii) Fused prochromosomes (iii) An aggregation of heterochromatin in salivary gland nuclei. *cf.* Heterochromatin

Chromocyte. — A pigment-cell.

Chromogen. — A cell substance which oxidises to form pigment.

Chromogene. — Lindegren's (1946) term for the locus of a gene. On this theory the gene is dual and consists of a chromogene (locus) to which cytogenes are attached; both chromogenes and cytogenes are self-duplicating but the latter multiply independently in the cytoplasm. *cf.* Protosome, Episome, Genosome.

Chromomeres. — The chromatin granules of characteristic size and position seen in the chromosome thread at prophase. These granules are possibly identical with genes.

Chromonema-ta. — The chromosome thread; the "optical single thread within the chromosome" (Nebel).

Chromophil, Chromophilic. — Staining heavily; staining easily.

Chromophobe, Chromophobic. — Difficult to stain.

Chromoplast, Chromatophore. — In plants, a pigmented plastid (particularly if not a chloroplast) ; in animals a pigment cell.

Chromosomal Chimaera. — A chimaera the components of which do not have the same chromosome number.

Chromosomal Fibres. — "Fibre bundles connecting the tiny granules called 'spindle spherules' (important parts of the centromere) with the poles. These chromosomal fibres have by many authors been regarded as intimately involved in chromosomal movement as traction fibres for the chromosomes" (OSTERGREN & PRAKKEN).

Chromosome Arm. — A segment between the spindle attachment and either end of the chromosome.

Chromosome Bridge. — A dicentric chromatid the two centromeres of which move towards opposite poles at the first division so that the chromatid remains as a 'bridge' between the anaphase chromosomes

Chromosome Complement — A collective term for the group of chromosomes in a single nucleus whether somatic or gametic.

Chromosome Complex. — A set of chromosomes having a given segmental arrangement.

Chromosome Cycle. — All the changes which take place in the chromosomes of an organism from fertilization to gametogenesis.

Chromosome Map. — A diagram of the relative position of the genes in a chromosome. *cf.* Cytogenetic Map

Chromosome Matrix. — A chromophobic membrane enclosing the chromosome proper.

Chromosome Number. — The number of chromosomes in the nucleus of a cell, the somatic number (2n) appertains to body cells and the gametic number (n) to sex cells.

Chromosomes. — Chromophilic bodies, typically constant in number in any particular species, into which the nucleus resolves itself during cell division.

Branched ———. Chromosomes in which the chromatids fork dichotomously, either at the spindle attachment or elsewhere (WHITE 1937)

Ring ———. A chromosome whose two ends are fused to form a continuous circle.

Chromosome Set. — The whole complement of chromosomes present in, or derived from, the nucleus of a gamete.

Chromosome Thread. — The thread, consisting of centromere, chromomeres, achromatic connective thread and, perhaps, pellicle at prophase, and constituting, as a spiral, the metaphase chromosome (DARLINGTON).

Chromosomin. — A special protein in cell nuclei, thought by some to be the principal constituent of chromosomes (others hold nucleoprotein to be the principal constituent).

Citrin. — Vitamin P

Clandestine Evolution. — An evolutionary change, or trend, brought about, in the first instance, by an alteration in the embryonic or larval stage which is followed by its inclusion in the adult as a result of neoteny or foetalization, caenogenesis

Cleavage — The cell divisions which transform a fertilized ovum into an embryo.

Cleavage Nucleus. — The nucleus of the fertilized animal ovum.

Cleavage Polyembryony. — Polyembryony brought about by the separation of the zygote or young embryo into two or more units.

Cleistogameon. — A species which, in part, reproduces by means of cleistogamy (CAMP & GILLY, 1942)

Cleistogamic, Cleistogamous. — With close fertilization, this taking place within the unopened flowers. Opp. Chasmogamic

Cleistogamy. — The state of having close fertilization, this taking place within the unopened flowers Opp. Chasmogamy.

Cleistogene. — A plant which bears cleistogamous flowers.

Cleistogeny. — The state of bearing cleistogamic flowers. Adj. **Cleistogenous.**

Climatic Race. — An ecotype which has arisen as a result of adaptation to a different climate from that in which the rest of the species grows.

Cline. — A geographical gradient in phenotypic characters (FORD). A general term covering populations within a species which show geographical or ecological variation. cf. Ecoclines and Geoclines.

Clone. — A collective name for all the plants asexually reproduced from a common ancestor.

Coefficient of Destruction. — The percentage of progeny which must normally be eliminated in order to keep the progeny at a given level (CARPENTER, 1938).

Coenobium. — Cenobium, q.v.

Coenocyte. — A multinucleate mass of protoplasm arising as a result of nuclear division without cytoplasmic division. cf. Syncytium.

Coenogamete. — A gamete with several nuclei.

Coenospecies. — The total sum of possible combinations of a genotype compound (TURESSON). A variable hybrid of two Linnean or ecospecies (CARPENTER, 1938).

Coenozygote. — The product of the fusion in fertilization of two coenogametes.

Cognation. — Kinship to a common pair of ancestors.

Coil. — See Spiral.

Coincidence. — The ratio of the number of double breaks found to the number of double breaks which should occur if there were no interference. This ratio is used as a measure of interference in the crossing-over of chromosomes.

Coition, Coitus. — Copulation, sexual intercourse.

Colchicine. — $C_{22}H_{25}O_6N$. An alkaloid obtained from *Colchicum autumnale* used in medicine for lowering the uric acid threshold of the kidney and in genetics to induce polyploidy. Colchicine also occurs in the tubers of *Gloriosa* spp. "In mitosis colchicine inactivates the spindle mechanism and delays the division of the centromeres. Prophase stages ordinarily show no irregularities. The nuclear membrane disappears but no spindle develops and the condensed chromosomes . . . form an irregular metaphase plate. After a few hours the centromeres divide, but the daughter chromosomes, in the absence of a spindle, do not pass to the poles . . A nuclear membrane forms about them and the number of chromosomes becomes doubled as a result of the longitudinal division" (BEAL, 1942)

Collateral Inheritance. — A term used to describe the appearance of characters in collateral members of a family, as when an uncle and a niece show the same character, inherited by the related individuals from a common ancestor. Collateral inheritance is characteristic of recessive characters which appear irregularly in contrast to dominant characters which do not skip a generation in inheritance (J Heredity).

Colostrum. — The milk which is produced at the very beginning of a lactation period and which contains more protein and minerals than normal milk.

Combining Ability. — The relative ability of a biotype to transmit desirable performance to its crosses (HAYES & IMMER).

General —— —— is "the average performance of a line in hybrid combination" and **Specific —— ——** is used to indicate "those cases in which certain combinations do relatively better or worse than would be expected on the basis of the average performance of the lines involved" (SPRAGUE & TATUM).

Commiscuum. — A group consisting of all the organisms which are capable of being intercrossed.

Communal Connubium. — A group of individuals within which mating is promiscuous.

Comparate Chiasmata. — Symmetrical chiasmata, *i.e.* chiasmata which are either reciprocal or complementary, *q.v.* Opp. Disparate Chiasmata

Comparium. — A commiscuum, *q.v.*

Compatible. — Readily capable of fertilization.

Complement. — A collective term for the group of chromosomes in a single nucleus whether somatic or gametic

Complementary Chiasmata. — Chiasmata formed between four chromatids in such a way that the first chiasma occurs between two of the chromatids and the second between their homologues.

Complementary Factor. — A factor which only in conjunction with one or more other genes, controls a particular character.

Complete Penetrance. — Said of a dominant gene whose presence in an organism always produces an effect on that organism, or of a recessive gene whose presence in the homozygous state always produces an effect. *See also* Penetrance and Incomplete Penetrance.

Complete Sex Linkage. — This occurs when the gene concerned is located on that portion of the X-choromosome which has no homologous segment in the Y-chromosome. A few cases are known of complete sex linkage where the gene concerned is carried on the short terminal portion of the Y-choromosome which has no homologous segment in the X-chromosome.

Compound Determiners. — Two or more genes which together make a particular character phenotypically evident.

Compound X-chromosomes. — A group of chromosomes which, in certain forms, acts in place of the usual X-chromosome. This group acts as a compound X during spermatogenesis (*e.g. Ascaris incurva* which has 8X + 1Y).

Conception. — Fertilization in animals, particularly in humans.

Condensation or Contraction, of the chromosome. The thickening shortening and spiralization of the chromatids during prophase (DARLINGTON).

Conditional Dominance. — Used of a gene which produces an effect in the heterozygous state but the homozygote of which is, as yet, unknown

Conditioned Dominance. — Dominance which is affected by the presence of modifying genes (dominigenes) *cf.* Fancier's Dominance.

Conditioned Reflex. — A reflex action which results from habit or experience on the part of the individual. *cf.* Unconditioned Reflex

Configuration. — An association of chromosomes at meiosis, segregating independently of other associations at anaphase (DARLINGTON).

Confusing Coloration. — A form of protective coloration which confuses the predator by having a different appearance according to whether its possessor is at rest or in motion.

Congenital. — Present at, or dating from, birth, but not, necessarily, inherited in the genetic sense.

Congression — The moving of the chromosomes into the equatorial region at metaphase.

Conjugant. — (1) A gamete at the time of fertilization. (ii) One of two pairing chromosomes at synapsis

Conjugation. — (i) Side-by-side association of homologous chromosomes at meiosis. (ii) Pairing of gametes or zygotes, or fusion of two nuclei.

Constriction — An unspiralised segment of fixed position in the metaphase chromosome (AGAR, DARLINGTON)

Constriction, Centric — The spindle attachment constriction.

Constriction, Nucleolar. — A secondary constriction determined by the organisation of the nucleolus (DARLINGTON).

Constriction, Primary. — The centromere

Constriction, Secondary. — One separating a satellite from the rest of the chromosome.

Constriction, Tertiary. — Any constriction other than the centromere (primary constriction) or one separating a satellite (secondary constriction) from the rest of the chromosome.

Contabescence. — Atrophy of anthers and pollen.

"Contact" Hypothesis. — The theory that chromosomes occasionally undergo illegitimate crossing-over between non-homologous sections, resulting in an interchange of blocks of genes (*cf* DOBZHANSKY, 1941).

Continuous Fibres — 'Fibres' which connect the two poles of a spindle, as distinct from chromosomal fibres and interzonal fibres, *q v*

Continuous Variations. — Those in which the variants differ from each other by infinitely small steps as opposed to discrete variations where the groups are distinct and there is no merging. Variations in height, weight, etc. are normally continuous, variations in number (eggs per bird, tubers per plant, etc.) are discrete.

Contraction. — *See* Condensation.

Convergence. — The evolution of similar structures produced by different means in different lines of descent

Convivium. — Convivum, *q.v.*

Convivum. — A group, within a species, which is prevented geographically from hybridization with the rest of the species although fertility has not been lost.

Co-orientation. — The relative orientation of the two centromeres on the spindle (DARLINGTON)

Copulation. — Coitus, sexual intercourse.

Core. — The endogenous sector of a periclinal chimaera.

Corolla — The interior perianth, composed of petals and often brightly coloured

Corolla-tube. — The basal portion of a corolla in which the individual petals are fused to form a tube, *e g* Primrose.

Corpora Albicantia. — Small white bodies arising from corpora lutea when ova liberated are not fertilized (HENDERSON).

Corpora Lutea — Yellow glandular bodies formed from the Graafian follicles, after the extrusion of the ova, in *Mammalia*.

Corpus Haemorrhagicum — A body formed from the ruptured Graafian follicle (after the escape of the ovum) by the closing of the cavity around the blood clot. The corpus haemorrhagicum is the first stage in the development of the corpus luteum.

Corpuscular System of Heredity. — The plastid system of heredity in which determinants, or units of heredity, are carried by the plastids. *cf* Nuclear System and Cytoplasmic System.

Correlation Coefficient. — *See* Appendix 1.

Coterminous. — Similar in geographic distribution

Cotypes. — The specimens on which the original description of a species was based (MAYR, 1942). *cf.* Holotype.

Coupling. — The state of having two linked recessive genes on one chromosome and their two dominant alleles on the other.

C.O.V. — Cross-over value, *q v.*

Cowper's Glands — The homologue, in the male, of the glands of Bartholin in the female. Cowper's glands are situated on either side of the urethra, into which their ducts open, and their function is probably to cleanse and neutralize the urethra before ejaculation

Creative Evolution — Evolution which follows a fore-ordained path.

Crescents — Part of the Golgi Apparatus, *q v.*

Crisscross Inheritance. — The scheme of inheritance whereby the female is normally the heterozygous carrier of a recessive sex-linked gene the effect of which is only evident in her sons.

Criss-crossing. — The continuous use of pure bred sires on alternate breeds. "Thus sows produced by crossing breeds A and B would be mated back to A Their daughters . . . would be mated to a B boar The gilts thus produced . . . would then be mated to an A boar" (LUSH, 1943).

Cross. — N. A hybrid; an individual whose parents differed genetically. V. To hybridize.

Cross Homology. — Residual homology, *q.v.*

Cross-incompatibility. — The inability of the gametes from two different individuals to unite although the individuals themselves are otherwise fertile.

Crossing-over. — An exchange of corresponding segments between the chromatids of homologous chromosomes.

    Double ——. — The production of a chromosome in which crossing-over has occurred twice; may be reciprocal or non-reciprocal as between chromatids at meiosis (STURTEVANT; DARLINGTON).

    Effective ——. — Crossing-over which is demonstrable by means of progeny tests.

    Illegitimate ——. — Crossing-over in a haploid or polyploid which is not a structural hybrid, between homologous and reduplicated segments of two chromosomes which, being structurally dissimilar as a whole, do not normally pair Determines secondary structural change (DARLINGTON). A physical exchange between non-homologous chromosomes or between non-corresponding segments of a single chromosome.

    Somatic ——. — An exchange of segments between homologous chromosomes at mitosis.

Crossover Region. — The segment of a chromosome which lies between any two specified gene loci.

Cross-over Suppressor. — Any gene inhibiting crossing-over.

Cross-over Unit. — A cross-over value (*q.v.*) of 1%.

Cross-over Value. — The sum of the two recombination classes in a backcross expressed as a percentage of the total offspring.

Cross-pollination. — The act of placing on the stigma of a flower, pollen derived from another plant not in the same clone

Cryptic Coloration. — Coloration which camouflages the individual so that it is less readily seen

Cryptic Contamination. — Contamination of a seed supply by outcrossing, the contamination not being evident in the immediate next generation because it is masked by dominance or by general similarity of the two parental types

Cryptogonomery. — This consists in the parent nuclei in hybrids retaining their individuality until the reduction division and separating at reduction.

Cryptomere. — (i) A gene which by itself has no visible effect but whose existence can be demonstrated by means of suitable crosses, *i e* a complementary factor. (ii) A recessive factor.

Cryptomerism. — The masking of characters due to recessiveness or to a complementary factor basis of inheritance (*see* cryptomere).

Cryptomitosis. — A type of division, found in *Protozoa*, in which a spindle is formed but no chromosomes appear, the chromatin agglomerating in the equatorial region in a single mass.

Cryptoplasm. — The non-granular portion of the cytoplasm.

Cryptorchid. — Having the testes within the abdominal cavity; an individual whose testes have not descended into the scrotum.

Cryptorchidism. — The condition which results from the failure of one or both testicles to descend into the scrotum.

C-tumour. — The characteristic swelling produced by plant tissues which have been treated with colchicine or some similar polyploiding substance.

Cull. — To remove, or discard, undesirable individuals from a family, breed, variety or other breeding unit, the equivalent, in animal breeding, of roguing in plant breeding

Cumulative Factors. — Non-allelomorphic factors affecting the same character and enhancing each other's effect; additive factors.

Cumulus Oophorus. — A small 'mound' of epithelial cells on which the ovum rests within the Graafian follicle.

Cutting. — A portion of a plant which is cut off and encouraged to form roots so as to produce a new plant.

Cyclosis. — The "streaming" of protoplasm within a cell

Cyesis. — Pregnancy, gestation; the period between fertilization and the birth of the offspring.

Cytaster. — An aster which is located in the cytoplasm outside the immediate nuclear zone.

Cytes. — Spermatocyte and oocyte stages in gametogenesis.

Cytoblast. — A nucleus; the most constant constituent of animal and plant cells which reproduces by mitosis and contains the chromosomes

Cytocentrum. — Central body, *q.v.*

Cytochrome. — An oxidisable pigment which is present in most cells.

Cytochylema. — Cell sap; the more fluid constituents of a cell.

Cytode. — A mass of protoplasm lacking a nucleus.

Cytodiaeresis. — Mitosis; the process of nuclear division in which daughter nuclei are formed each having a chromosome complement similar to that of the original nucleus. For details *see* under Mitosis

Cytogamy. — Conjugation, union, or fusion of cells.

Cytogene. — *See* under Chromogene

Cytogenesis. — The formation, reproduction or development of cells. Adj **Cytogenetic.**

Cytogenetic Map. — A map showing the actual positions of the genes within the physical chromosome, as distinct from a chromosome map which merely shows the position of the genes relative to each other.

Cytogenetics. — The interpretation of the phenomena of heredity in terms of cell structures.

Cytokinesis. — The division of the cytoplasm of a cell.

Cytological Interference. — The effect whereby the formation of one chiasma lessens the probability of the occurrence of another in its vicinity.

Cytology. — The study of the structure, physiology, development and reproduction of cells.

Cytolymph. — Cell sap; the more fluid constituents of a cell

Cytolysin. — A substance which brings about cell dissolution

Cytolysis. — Cell dissolution.

Cytomere. — (i) The cytoplasm of a sperm. (ii) Plastomere, *q v.*

Cytomicrosome. — A microsome occurring in the cytoplasm.

Cytomitome. — The cytoplasmic threadwork in contradistinction to the nuclear threadwork (FLEMMING; WILSON).

Cytomorphosis. — A general term for the changes occurring in cell substances during differentiation, development and senescence of the cell

Cytoplasm. — The whole of the protoplasm of a cell excluding the nucleus. Adj. **Cytoplasmic.**

Cytoplasmic Inheritance. — The transmission of hereditary characters by the cytoplasm as distinct from transmission by genes situated at definite loci on the chromosomes. Also called the "molecular" system of heredity *cf.* Nuclear System and Corpuscular System

Cytoreticulum. — Cytomitome, *q v*

Cytosome. — The cytoplasm of a single cell.

Cytothesis. — Cell repair.

Cytula. — A fertilized ovum, zygote.

Dam. — The female parent (animal breeding).

Darwinism. — DARWIN's theory that species originate by the constant selection of beneficial adaptations, as a result of the effect of natural selection working on the slight variations that occur.

Darwin's Theory of Sexual Selection. — *See* under Selection, Darwin's Theory of Sexual.

Dauermodification. — A phenomenon in which environmentally produced modification of an organism reappears in a lessening degree for one or more subsequent generations.

Daughter Chromosome. — A half chromosome during anaphase. *See* under Chromatid.

DCR. — Double cross-overs. *See* under Crossing-over.

Decidua. — (1) The mucous membrane of the uterus during pregnancy and at the time when it is shed (at parturition). (ii) Afterbirth.

Deconjugation. — Abnormally early separation of the paired homologous chromosomes before the end of prophase in meiosis.

Deficiency. — The loss of a segment of a chromosome from the genom.

Definitive Nucleus. — A nucleus formed in the embryo-sac by the fusion of the two polar nuclei. The definitive nucleus later fuses with a male nucleus to form the triploid endosperm nucleus.

Degeneration. — (i) Devolution. (ii) Deterioration of a variety (usually under conditions of commercial cultivation).

Dehydroandrosterone. — This substance appears to be a metabolic product of testosterone; it occurs in urine (both male and female) and has androgenic activity.

7-Dehydrocholesterol. — Vitamin D_3.

Delayed Dominant. — Used of a character which only appears to the exclusion of its alternative allele late in ontogeny.

Deletion. — A deficiency in which an internal segment of chromosome is missing, as distinct from a terminal segment.

Deletion Heterozygote. — An individual heterozygous for the absence of an internal segment of one of its chromosomes.

Deme. — Any specified assemblage of taxonomically closely related individuals (GILMOUR & GREGOR).

Derivative Hybrid. — A hybrid arising from a cross between two hybrids.

Desmones. — Hormones which are supposed to induce mitosis (FISCHER, 1945).

Desoxycorticosterone — A steroid, produced by the suprarenal cortex which has a progesterone-like action and possibly androgenic properties also.

Desynapsis. — The falling apart of synapsing chromosomes before metaphase (synapsis having first occurred during the meiotic prophase).

Detachment. — The separation of a single X-chromosome from attached X-chromosomes, as a result of crossing-over between the X and Y-chromosomes near the centromere.

Determinate Variation. — Orthogenesis, *q.v*

Determiner, Determinant. — Archaic synonyms for gene.

Deuterotoky. — Parthenogenesis in which both males and females are formed.

Deuthyalosome. — The nucleus of the immature ovum after the second meiotic division.

Deviation. — (i) A variation from the mean. (ii) An evolutionary change arising in the middle of ontogeny.

Deviation, Progressive. — The progressive divergence of an animal, during its ontogeny, from the ontogenetic stages of the ancestor.

Deviation, Standard. — *See* Appendix 1.

Devolution. — Retrogressive evolution.

Diad. — (i) Two daughter cells arising from a spore mothercell, as a result of meiotic irregularities, instead of a tetrad. (ii) An univalent chromosome (two chromatids) at meiosis.

Diadelphous. — Having the filaments of the stamens fused into two bundles, or having one stamen solitary and the remainder fused.

Diagenic. — Of a genetic character passing from male to male through the female by way of the sex chromosome.

Diakinesis. — The later stages in the prophase of meiosis between diplotene and prometaphase and immediately prior to the dissolution of the nuclear membrane.

Diallel Crossing. — (i) The crossing of different (inbred) lines together in pairs. (ii) A method of comparing the breeding value of two males by breeding them at different times to the same females and comparing the average performance of the progenies

Dialycarpic. — Having two or more carpels, all separate *i e* apocarpic.

Dialypetalous. — Polypetalous; having several distinct (separate) petals.

Diandric. — Of a genetic character. passing from female to female through the male by means of the sex chromosome (birds and moths)

Diarch. — A type of anastral spindle in higher plants that is bipolar from the beginning (STRASBURGER; WILSON).

Diaschistic. — Of bivalents that are said to divide transversely at the first division, this is owing to the chromosomes being united by a single terminal or nearly terminal chiasma (FARMER & MOORE, DARLINGTON).

Diastem — The plane of mitotic division of a cell

Diaster. — The stage at the end of mitosis or meiosis when the daughter chromosomes are grouped near the poles of the spindle.

Dibasic. — Allopolyploid, *q.v.*

Dicaryotic. — Dikaryotic, *q.v.*

Dicentric. — Having two centromeres.

Dichlamidius Chimaera. — A periclinal chimaera in which the genetically distinct peripheral tissue is two layers of cells thick.

Dichlamydeous Chimaera. — Dichlamidius, *q.v*

2, 4-Dichlorophenoxyacetic Acid. — A growth regulating substance which has been used with considerable effect at low concentrations in flower induction. At higher concentrations this substance is used as a selective herbicide (*cf.* OVERBEEK, 1945).

Dichogamy. — The absence of simultaneous maturation of stamens and stigmas in a flower so that their ripening does not overlap and cross-pollination is ensured. Adj. **Dichogamous.**

Diclinous. — Having staminate and pistillate flowers either on the same plant or on different plants.

Dictyate Stage. — Dictyotic stage, *q v.*

Dictyokinesis. — The division of the Golgi apparatus at mitosis and the even distribution of dictyosomes between the daughter cells.

Dictyosome. — One of the elements which make up the Golgi apparatus.

Dictyotic Stage. — The period when the chromosomes are transformed into the nuclear reticulum.

Didiploid. — An autotetraploid, autopolyploid or duplicational polyploid; a tetraploid whose somatic nuclei contain four similar sets of chromosomes.

Didynamous. — Having only four stamens of which two are short and two are long.

Dienoestrol. — A synthetic oestrogenic hormone more powerful than the natural product.

Dientomophily. — The state of having some members of the species adapted for pollination by one species of insect whilst others are pollinated by a different species.

Differential Affinity. — The differential attraction which exists between chromosomes showing residual homology as compared with truly homologous chromosomes, so that though two chromosomes with residual homology can pair, they will not do so in the presence of the true homologue of either of them.

Differential and Interference Distances. — These are, respectively, the distance between the centromere and the mean position of the proximal chiasma, and the mean distance between the proximal or first and the next proximal or second chiasma (MATHER, 1940).

Differential Precocity. — *See* under Precocity

Differential Segment. — A segment of a chromosome which has no exact equivalent in the other member of the bivalent. Opp. Pairing Segment.

Differentiation. — The specialization of cells and tissues which takes place during the growth of an embryo and which eventually enables the various tissues to function as the specialized organs which make up the adult organism.

Digametic. — Having gametes of two classes, male and female. **N. Digamy.**

Digenesis. — Alternation of generations, an alternation of a sexual with an asexual form, or, cytologically, the alternation of a haploid with a diploid stage

Digeneutic. — Having two breeding seasons per year.

Digenic. — Controlled by two genes.

Digenomic Species. — A species whose gametes all carry two sets of chromosomes, *i e.* a tetraploid species.

Digynous. — With two carpels.

Dihaploid. — An individual derived from a tetraploid but carrying only half the normal tetraploid chromosome complement

Diheterozygote. — An organism heterozygous for two pairs of genes; a dihybrid.

Dihybrid. — A cross between parents differing in two genes, or differing in two specified genes

Dihydroxystilbene. — A synthetic oestrogen.

Dikaryotic Hybrid. — A 'hybrid' whose cells carry two un-fused haploid nuclei, as occurs in certain fungi

Diluting Factor. — A minor factor which, by itself, has no effect but which lessens the effect of a major factor.

Dimegaly. — Having two types of egg, or of sperm, one larger than the other.

Dimeric. — Carrying dominant genes at both of two duplicate loci. *cf.* Monomeric

Diminution. — The elimination of a portion of the chromosome complement during nuclear division with the result that the daughter nucleus is deficient in this part.

Dimonoecious. — Having perfect (bisexual) flowers as well as pistillate and staminate flowers on the one plant.

Dimorphism — (i) The occurrence of two distinct forms within a species *See* Polymorphism. (ii) The production of two distinct types of flower on the one plant.

Dinergatandromorph. — A 'soldier-male' type of sex mosaic which occurs in ants.

Dioecious. — Having male and female flowers on separate unisexual plants.

Dioestrum, Dioestrus. — The resting interval between heat periods (oestrus) in animals.

Di-oval Twins. — Dizygotic, fraternal, or dissimilar twins, *i e* those arising from two distinct ova

Diphyletic. — Having two lines of descent.

Diplo-. — The term diplo-, followed by a symbol designating a particular chromosome, indicates an individual in whose somatic cells both members of this particular chromosome-pair are present. Diplo- is used to distinguish individuals of this type from haplo- and triplo- (*q v*) individuals.

Diplobiont. — A plant which has two flowering periods each year.

Diplobivalent. — A diplochromosome (*q v.*) bivalent comprising eight chromatids.

Diplochromosome. — A chromosome which has divided once more often than it normally does in relation to its centromere (*cf.* attached X in *Drosophila melanogaster*) (WHITE; DARLINGTON).

Diplochlamydeous Chimaera. — A periclinal chimaera in which the peripheral constituent is two layers of cells thick.

Diplo-haploid Twinning. — A form of polyembryony in which one embryo is diploid and the other haploid.

Diploid — (1) The somatic number of chromosomes (2n) as opposed to the gametic (haploid) number (n). (ii) An organism whose somatic nuclei have two sets of chromosomes.

Diploid Apogamety. — Euapogamy, diploid apogamy, q v.

Diploid Apogamy. — The formation of a diploid sporophyte from a gametophyte without fertilization having occurred, euapogamy.

Diploid, Functional. — An allopolyploid which behaves as a diploid in segregation (DARLINGTON).

Diploid Organism. — An individual possessing two haploid sets of chromosomes in all of its somatic nuclei.

Diploid Parthenogenesis. — *See* under Parthenogenesis

Diploid Set of Chromosomes. — A complement of chromosomes which consists of two equal haploid groups.

Diploidisation. — A form of nuclear division, found in certain fungi, by which the chromosome number is doubled.

Diplokaryotic. — Possessing double the usual diploid number of chromosomes; tetraploid.

Diplonema. — The double chromosome thread at the diplotene stage in meiosis.

Diplont. — An organism during the diploid phase of its life-cycle. Opp. Haplont.

Diplontic Sterility. — Sterility due to the production of gametes which form inviable zygotes; zygotic sterility.

Diplophase. — (i) Diplotene, q v (ii) The stage in the life-cycle of an organism when the nuclei contain the diploid number of chromosomes

Diplosis. — A doubling of the gametic chromosome number.

Diplosome. — (i) A paired heterosome (ii) A double centrosome outside the nuclear membrane.

Diplospory. — The production of unreduced spores from archesporial tissues.

Diplotene. — The stage of meiosis following pachytene, at which the four chromatids in each bivalent move apart in two pairs but the two pairs remain adherent in the region of chiasmata.

Diprosopus. — A foetal monster which is characterized by the presence of two faces.

Dipygus. — A foetal abnormality characterized by a double pelvis.

Disc Floret. — A regular tubular floret typically found in the inner portion of a capitulum.

Discontinuous Variation. — A mutation, or sudden heritable variation

Discrete Variations. — *See* under Continuous Variations

Disease Garden. — A nursery in which plants can be grown under optimum conditions for any or several particular diseases as a means of studying resistance

Disjunction — The moving apart of chromosomes at anaphase.

Dislocated Segments. — Homologous pairs of segments in a different linear sequence from other segments in a structural hybrid (DARLINGTON).

Dislocation. — Structural change, *q.v.*

Disomaty. — The production of somatic nuclei with twice the normal somatic chromosome number, tetraploidy

Disome. — A diploid chromosome complement, a chromosome set having paired members, as in normal somatic tissue.

Disomic. — Of two homologous chromosomes, or genes

Disparate Chiasmata. — Chiasmata which produce an asymmetrical relationship between chromatids in that the second chiasma does not restore the relationship altered by the first. Opp. Comparate Chiasmata

Dispermic Fertilization, Dispermy. — Fertilization of an ovum by two spermatozoa

Dispireme. — The stage of karyokinesis in which the spireme thread has formed in both daughter nuclei

Dissogeny. — Dissogony, *q.v.*

Dissogony. — Having two periods of sexual maturity during the life cycle, one during the larval stage and the other during adulthood.

Distal. — Of a chromosome, that part which is furthest from the centromere.

Distal Chiasma. — (i) A chiasma formed in that portion of a chromosome which is distal to an inversion loop *i e* so that the loop lies between the chiasma and the centromere (ii) A chiasma formed further away from the centromere than a particular other chiasma.

Ditokous. — Producing two young (or eggs) at a time.

d/i Values. — The ratio of differential distance to interference distance. *See* Differential and Interference Distances.

Dizygotic. — (Generally of twins) originating from two fertilized eggs.

Dollo's Law of Irreversibility. — Evolution is reversible in that structures or functions once gained may be lost, but irreversible in that structures or functions once lost can never be regained (NEEDHAM)

Dominance. — See under Dominant, Irregular ——, Mock ——, Conditional ——, Conditioned ——, Partial ——, Semi ——, Fancier's ——

Dominance, Hypothesis of Antithetical — In hybrids between extremely diverse parents, natural selection will tend to encourage those modifiers favouring one parental extreme or the other and suppressing intermediates (ANDERSON & ERICKSON)

Dominant Character — A character possessed by one parent of a hybrid which appears in the F_1 to the exclusion of the allelic character from the other parent By extension, the gene controlling such a character is said to be dominant or to show dominance Dominance may be complete, incomplete (partial) or absent. Where the character is measurable the degree of dominance may be expressed as $100\dfrac{h}{d}$ where h is the deviation of the heterozygote from the mean of the two homozygotes and d is half the difference between the two homozygotes.

Dominigenes. — Modifying genes which are able to modify the dominance of another gene.

Donor Parent — That parent from which, by backcrossing, one or more genes are transferred to the backcross parent.

Dosage Compensation. — The effect whereby a single dose of a sex-linked gene has the same developmental result in the heterogametic sex as a double dose has in the homogametic sex

Dosage Indifference. — The effect whereby in certain organisms the male may possess several Y-chromosomes, or none at all, without upsetting the genetic balance of the individual.

Double Cross. — Double F_1, q v

Double Diploid — Allotetraploid, q v.

Double Dominants. — Two dominant, non-allelic factors which together produce a certain phenotypic character which does not appear in the absence of either or of both of them; dominant complementary factors

Double F_1. — A cross between two F_1s such that the hybrid has all four grand-parents different.

Double Haploid. — A diploid plant carrying a chromosome set from each of two distinct species.

Double Reduction. — The occurrence of a reductional division at both (meiotic) divisions in regard to particular parts of chromosomes, possible in some hybrids and polyploids; hence "equational exceptions" (DARLINGTON; HALDANE).

Double Tetraploid. — An octoploid carrying in its somatic nuclei four genoms from one species and four genoms from another distinct species.

Drift — Change in the relative frequency of two alleles in a population, by chance, as distinct from such change under selection.

Duplex. — (i) Of a diploid· homozygous for a given dominant gene (AA) (ii) Of a triploid having two doses of a given dominant gene and one of its recessive allele (AAa). (iii) Of a tetraploid having two doses of a given dominant gene (AAaa).

Duplicate Genes. — Identical genes but situated at different loci and showing no cumulative effect

Duplication. — The occurrence of one segment of a chromosome twice in the same complement.

Duplicational Polyploid. — An organism having more than two homologous sets of chromosomes in its body cells derived from a single parent species; an autopolyploid, or autotetraploid.

Dyad. — Diad, q v

Dysgenesis. — Infertility, especially between hybrids which are fertile with members of either parent line (BEADNELL).

Dysgenic. — Tending to impair the hereditary qualities of the human race Opp Eugenic.

Dysploid. — Aneuploid, q v.

Dysploidion. — A species composed of the morphologically similar members of a dysploid series, the individuals of which are sexually reproductive (CAMP & GILLY).

Dysteleology. — The supposition that nature (and especially organic evolution) lacks any foreordained direction or purpose

Dystokia, Dystocia. — Abnormaly painful and difficult parturition.

Dystrophy. — Perforation of the perianth by insects seeking nectar so that the insects do not serve as pollinating agents.

E₁, E₂, E₃. — First, second and third generations following irradiation with X-rays.

Ecad. — A plant type which has resulted from adaptation to the selective effect of environment.

Eccyesis. — Extra-uterine growth of the foetus (*e.g* in a Fallopian tube), ectopic gestation.

Ecobiotic Adaptation. — Adaptation to a particular mode of life within a habitat (HUXLEY).

Ecoclimatic Adaptation. — Adaptation to the broad physical and climatic features of any particular region

Ecoclines. — The graduations of variation produced within a species by its reaction to the different ecological zones in which it occurs. *cf* Cline and Geocline

Ecogeographical Divergence. — The evolution from a single ancestral form of two or more different forms each in a different geographical area and each adapted to the local peculiarities of its particular area

Ecological Divergence. — Adaptation to different ecological conditions resulting in the evolution of divergent types. Ecological divergence includes ecobiotic adaptation, ecoclimatic adaptation, ecogeographical adaptation (or divergence) and ecotopic adaptation, *q.v.*

Ecological Isolation. — Separation of groups due to change in habit or habitat (especially of insects changing their food habits and thus becoming isolated from the rest of the species).

Ecological Rules. — *See* under Allen, Bergmann, Gloger, Rensch.

Ecology. — The relationship between living organisms and their environment.

Ecophene. — Ecad, *q.v.*

Ecophenotype. — A habitat form

Ecoproterandry. — The maturing of male flowers before the female flowers.

Ecoproterogyny. — The maturing of female flowers before the male flowers.

Ecospecies, Ecotype — A distinct race resulting from the selective action of a particular environment. More strictly "ecotype" is "used as an ecological sub-unit to cover the product arising as a result of the genotypical response of an eco-species to a particular habitat" and 'ecospecies" is "the genotype compound narrowed down to the ecological combination-limit" (TURESSON).

Ecotopic Adaptation. — Adaptation to the detailed features of a particular type of habitat within a region (HUXLEY).

Ecotype. — *See* under Ecospecies

Ectogenesis. — The artificial development of an embryo by culture in vitro

Ectogeny. — Metaxenia; the physiological effect of pollen on the maternal tissues

Ectopic Gestation. — Extra-uterine growth of the foetus, eccyesis.

Ectoplasm — Non-granular, peripheral cytoplasm; exoplasm.

Ectoplast. — Ectoplasm, *q.v*

Ectosarc. — Ectoplasm, *q v.*

Ectosomes. — Specific cytoplasmic granules characteristic of the primordial germ-cells and stem-cells in copepods A form of 'germ-cell determinant' (HAECKER, WILSON)

Ectosphere. — The peripheral region of the centrosphere.

Egg. — The female gamete in animals, ovum

Ejaculatory Ducts. — Small slit-like openings in the floor of the urethra, through which the spermatozoa pass from the vasa deferentia during ejaculation

Elaioplast. — An oil-producing plastid.

Electosomes. — A general term applied to chondriosomes (mitochondria) considered as centres of specific chemical action (REGAUD, WILSON)

Emasculation. — (i) The removal of the anthers from a bud or flower. (ii) Castration.

Emasculatome. — An instrument, generally consisting of double-hinged pincers, used in emasculation for crushing the spermatic cord

Emboitement. — Encasement, *q v.*

Embryo. — The non-self-supporting immature organism formed from the zygote by segmentation and differentiation

Embryo-cell. — One of two cells formed from first division of fertilized egg in certain plants, developing later into embryo, the other developing into suspensor (HENDERSON).

Embryo Culture. — A method of inducing growth of embryos artificially. The technique is of value in obtaining progeny from interspecific crosses in which the partially developed embryos normally abort, and it consists in excising the young embryos under aseptic conditions and placing them on suitable nutrient media.

Embryogeny. — The development of a zygote into an embryo.

Embryology. — The study of embryos and of anything affecting embryos.

Embryonic. — Of cells not differentiated nor specialized.

Embryo-sac. — The female gametophyte formed by division of the megaspore.

Embryo-sac Mother-cell. — A cell of hypodermal origin which undergoes a tetrad division to form four cells one of which develops into the embryo-sac or megaspore

E-M-C. — Embryo-sac Mother-cell, *q v*

Emmenin. — An oestrogen, probably oestriol glucuronide, present in the placenta.

Encasement. — An extension of the theory of preformation which supposed that, if the seed contained a complete miniature of the organism of the next generation, this miniature must itself contain seed, *i e.* miniatures of the organisms of a generation still further ahead and so *ad infinitum*

Enchylema. — The cell sap, the more fluid constituents of a cell.

Endemic. — Confined to a small section of the country, *e.g.* endemic species

Endogamy. — (i) Self-pollination (ii) Inbreeding. (iii) union of two sister female gametes

Endogenous. — Of internal origin; growing from within

Endomitosis. — A division process in which chromosome doubling occurs unaccompanied by nuclear division, spindle formation or chromosome movement and in which the nuclear membrane remains intact.

Endomixis. — A process of self-fertilization sometimes seen in *Paramaecium*, in which the sperm and egg nuclei, from the one individual, unite.

Endoplasm. — The granular inner portion of the cytoplasm; endosarc.

Endopolyploidy. — The division, or repeated division, of the chromosomes of a cell without the nucleus or the cell itself dividing.

Endosarc. — Endoplasm, *q v.*

Endosome. — A karyosome; a vague term meaning a chromosome, a special form of nucleolus or even a nucleus.

Endosperm. — Triploid nutritive tissue arising by "double fertilization" by a second male nucleus of two of the eight nuclei of the embryo-sac.

Energic Nucleus. — A nucleus which is not dividing; resting nucleus.

Energic Stage. — Metabolic stage, *q v.*

Energid. — The nucleus and cytoplasm of a single cell.

Enneaploid. — Having nine times the haploid number of chromosomes.

Entelechy. — A hypothetical principle controlling purposive adaptation and evolution.

Entomogamous. — Pollinated by insects

Entomophilous. — Pollinated by insects.

Entoplasm — Endoplasm, *q v*

Entosphere. — The central portion of the centrosphere.

Enucleate — Without a nucleus by reason of its removal by mechanical means.

Enucleation. — Removal of the corpus luteum.

Environment. — The collective term for all the influences affecting the life, growth, health and activity of organisms

Environmental Variation. — An acquired character· a non-heritable variation caused by the reaction of the individual to an environmental change.

Epacme. — The phase in the development of a group, species or individual when vigour is still increscent.

Epharmonic Convergence. — Morphological and anatomical similarity between systematically unrelated, or only distantly related, plants

Epharmosis. — Organic adaptation to a changed environment.

Epibiotic Species. — Endemic species that are relics of a "lost" flora and compose a minor portion of the biota of most regions (CAIN, 1944)

Epididymis (pl. Epididymi). — A coiled duct of variable length (from a few feet to several hundred feet, according to species) into which the developing spermatozoa are conveyed from the seminiferous tubules and efferent ducts of the testis. Spermatozoa pass through the epididymi to the vasa deferentia and thence to the urethra.

Epigamic. — (i) Of colouring, plumage, etc.; attractive to the other sex. (ii) Promoting the union of gametes.

Epigamic Selection. — *See* under Selection, Epigamic.

Epigenesis. — The hypothesis that an embryo is a new creation which develops by gradual differentiation, as against the concept of preformation, that the individual is present in miniature, in the embryo and that the adult is produced merely by expansion.

Epigenetics. — The study of the causal mechanisms governing the processes by which the genes of the genotype bring about phenotypic effects (*cf.* WADDINGTON, 1942).

Epigenotype. — The complex of developmental processes linking the genotype with the resulting phenotype (*cf.* WADDINGTON, 1942).

Episematic Coloration. — Coloration used for purposes of recognition.

Episomes. — Minute physical entities supposed to be attached to the gene base (*see* protosome) to give the characteristic action of the gene, such action being the result of the interaction of the gene base with its episome or episomes. *cf.* Cytogene (under Chromogene).

Epistasis. — Dominance of one factor over another, the two not being allelic. Such a dominant factor is said to be **epistatic** and the non-allelomorphic recessive, **hypostatic.**

Epistasy. — (i) Epistasis. (ii) The state when one of two related types has undergone a greater degree of modification in phylogeny than the other.

Epistatic. — Dominant but non-allelomorphic; *see* Epistasis.

Equation Division. — The nonreduction division in meiosis; the homeotypic division.

Equatorial Plate. — The group of metaphase chromosomes lying at the equator of the spindle during nuclear division.

Equilenin. — $C_{18}H_{18}O_2$. A hormone found in the urine of pregnant mares.

Ergastic. — Of non-living metabolic products in a cell, such as oil globules, oxalates, etc.

Ergastoplasm. — Archiplasm, *q.v.*

Ergatomorphic Male. — A sex-mosaic which occurs in ants and which typically consists in the insect having the head, thorax and gaster predominantly worker or female, and the genetalia and antennae male. E-M-s are sometimes described as antero-lateral gynandromorphs or intersexes.

Ergines. — Organic biocatalyzers including enzymes, ergones, vitamins and hormones.

Ergone. — A term used to denote any substance with vitamin-like or hormonic properties which cannot, with certainty, be classed either as a vitamin or a hormone.

Ergosterol. — Pro-vitamin D, $C_{28}H_{44}O$ Vitamin D, the anti-rachitic vitamin, is formed from ergosterol by irradiation with ultraviolet light.

Errera's Law. — A cellular membrane at the moment of its formation tends to assume the form which would be assumed, under the same conditions, by a liquid film destitute of weight.

Erythrophilous. — Readily stainable with red dyes (as opposed to blue or green).

Escape. — An apparently wild plant which is, in reality, not truly wild, its presence being merely due to cultivation of this type at an earlier date in the vicinity

Estrogens. — Oestrogens, *q v*

Estrus. — Oestrus, *q v*

Etheogenesis, Ethiogenesis — Male parthenogenesis, the formation of an organism from a male gamete without fertilization having taken place.

Ethnobiology. — The study of the relations between man (especially primitive man) and his surrounding animal and vegetable life

Ethnobotany. — The study of the relations between man (especially primitive man) and his surrounding vegetation.

Ethnozoology. — The study of the relations between man (especially primitive man) and his surrounding animal life.

Ethological — Appertaining to custom, habit, or "behaviour pattern" (*cf.* MAYR, 1942)

Euapogamy. — The formation of a diploid sporophyte from a gametophyte without fertilization having occurred; diploid apogamy.

Euchromatic. — Of a chromosome, or portion of a chromosome staining less deeply (and presumed to consist of genetically active material) *cf* Heterochromatic.

Euchromatin. — *See* under Heterochromatin

Euchromocentre. — The heterochromatin on either side of the centric constriction.

Euchromosome. — An autosome; a normal chromosome, as opposed to a heterosome

Eugenic. — Tending to improve the human race

Eugenics — The application of the principles of genetics to the improvement of a race (especially of humans).

Eugenic Prognosis. — An estimate of the probability of a given disease or defect being inherited (BLACKER, 1934).

Euhermaphrodite. — A normal hermaphrodite plant in which both anthers and gynoecia are well developed in all flowers.

Eumitosis. — Typical mitosis.

Eumitotic. — Anaschistic, *q.v.*

Euphemeral. — Of flowers: lasting not more than 24 hours.

Euploid. — A polyploid whose chromosome number is an exact multiple of the haploid number of the species from which it arose.

Euploid Polyembryony. — Multiple embryos which give rise to haploids as well as polyploids.

Eupyrene. — Normal (as applied to spermatozoa).

Euryplastic. — Having considerable modificational plasticity, *q.v.* N. Euryplasty.

Eutelegenesis. — The use of artificial insemination for the improvement of the race.

Euthenic. — Tending to produce better conditions for people to live in, but not necessarily tending to produce people who can hand on this improvement by heredity (J. Heredity).

Exine. — *See* Extine.

Exogamy. — Conjugation between gametes of different ancestry; outbreeding.

Exogenous. — Arising from external tissues.

Exogynous. — With the style longer than the corolla and projecting beyond it.

Exoplasm. — Non-granular, peripheral cytoplasm; ectoplasm.

Explosive Speciation. — The rapid production, within the one locality, of a number of new species from a single species.

Expressivity. — The phenotypic degree of expression of a gene; a measure of the amount of effect caused by a gene. *cf.* Penetrance.

Expressivity, Heterozygous. — The degree of dominance or lack of dominance shown by a gene in the heterozygous state. Full heterozygous expressivity is the equivalent of full dominance, absence of heterozygous expressivity is the same as complete recessiveness.

Expressivity, Reduced. — The occurrence, within one genotype, of individuals showing a reduced manifestation of any particular gene or genes.

Exserted. — Of stamens: projecting beyond the corolla.

Extension Factor. — A factor (gene) which extends the action of a primary factor. Thus, in mammalian genetics, black or brown pigments restricted chiefly to the eye, become "extended" throughout the coat in black or brown varieties (J. Heredity).

Extine. — The outer membrane of a pollen grain.

Extramedial Hybridity Quotient. — A measurement of the extent to which the hybrid departs from the mean between the parents

Extramedial Response to Hybridity. — The extent to which the hybrid departs from the mean between the two parents.

F_1, F_2, F_3. — First, second and third generations, respectively, following a cross.

Double F_1. — A cross between two F_1s such that the hybrid has all four grand-parents different.

F_2 Ratios. — The expected proportion of other types to the bottom recessive in F_2 is found by calculating 4^n where n is number of factors involved. In a monofactorial cross $4^n = 4$ and the expected ratio is 3·1, with 2 factors $4^n = 16$ and the ratio is 15·1, with three factors $4^n = 64$ and the ratio is 63.1, etc.

Factor. — A unit occupying a fixed chromosomal locus and governing, or affecting, the transmission and development of a heritable character, gene.

Factor-pair. — *See* Allelomorph.

Fallopian Tube. — The first portion of the Mullerian duct in mammals which conveys ova from the peritoneal cavity to the uterus The upper portion of the oviduct.

Familial. — In the clinical sense· transmitted in families but with no unbroken continuity from generation to generation

Family. — (Animal breeding.) A group of individuals within a breed, all of which have pedigrees which trace directly in the female line to a common ancestress called the foundress of the family. At times used in reference to the male line of descent, in which case it is used interchangeably with line of breeding (WINTERS).

Fancier's Dominance. — Dominance built up by selection (especially in such characters as coat colour and bizarre appearances), such dominance breaks down if crossed and back-crossed with a variety which has not undergone such selection *cf*. Conditioned Dominance.

Farina. — An obsolete synonym for pollen.

Fatuoids. — A group of three types of oat mutants which resemble *Avena fatua*.

Fecundation. — Fertilization.

Female Pronucleus. — The nucleus of a female gamete.

Feral. — Wild (*i.e.* not cultivated).

Fertile — Capable of producing viable seeds, or offspring

Fertilization. — The fusion of two gametes, male and female, to form a zygote

Fertilization Cone — A small conical projection which is protruded from the surface of certain eggs at the point of contact with the sperm.

Fertilization Membrane. — A membrane which grows outward from the point of contact of egg and sperm and which rapidly covers the whole egg surface

Fertilizin. — A soluble substance produced by the egg and assumed to play an essential part in fertilization as a chemical link between egg and sperm (LILLIE, WILSON).

Fetus. — Foetus, *q v*

Filament. — The stalk on which an anther is borne.

Filial Generations. — F_1, F_2, F_3 etc., *q.v.*

Filial Regression. — The tendency of offspring of outstanding parentage to revert to average for species (HENDERSON).

Finalism. — The concept that the world (or the universe) has a definite purposive goal.

First Division. — The earlier of the two meiotic divisions, often called the heterotypic or reduction division.

Fission. — (i) Asexual division of a unicellular organism into two (ii) Division of a nucleus without, apparently, any mechanism for ensuring an equal distribution of homologous chromosomes.

Fixation. — The process of killing and coagulating a cell by means of some chemical or physical agency

Fixed. — Of a character, race, variety, etc pure-breeding, homozygous

Floret. — A small flower, usually in a clustered inflorescence

Foetalization — The prolongation into post-natal or adult life of foetal characters of remote ancestors

Foetus. — An embryo in utero or before hatching from an egg

Folic Acid. — One of the components of the vitamin B_2 complex. Folic acid prevents anaemia and leucopenia in chicks.

Follicular Hormone. — A female sex hormone formed by the ovarian follicles

Food Pollen. — Pollen formed for the purpose of attracting insects and which is often infertile

Fractionation (of a gene). — The breaking up of a gene into sub-units during segregation, a process which BATESON believed might occur. "I am satisfied that they (the genes)

may occasionally undergo a quantitative disintegration, with
the consequence that varieties are produced intermediate between the integral varieties from which they were derived"
cf. Step Allelomorphism.

Fracture. — The breaking of a chromosome into a centric
portion and one or more acentric portions, which do not
rejoin.

Fragmentation. — Division of a nucleus by fission; amitosis

Fraternal Twins. — Dizygotic individuals from a single birth;
twins, each of which arose from a separate ovum

Freemartin. — An intersex caused by the action of the sex
hormones of a male twin on its twin female foetus as a result
of anastomosis of placental blood vessels.

Fructification. — Production of fruit

Fusion Nucleus — The product of the fusion of the two polar
nuclei This, after fusing with a male nucleus, gives rise to
the endosperm.

G_1, G_2, G_3. — First, second and third self-bred generations.

Galton's Law. — An individual derives his characters as follows 1/4 from each parent, 1/16 from each grand-parent, 1/64 from each great-grand-parent, and so on.

Gametangium. — Any structure in which gametes are formed.

Gametes. — Cells, typically of meiotic origin, formed in the sexual organs, or their equivalent, and specialized for fertilization.

Gametic Incompatibility. — A form of homomorphic incompatibility ($q v.$) in which the incompatibility reaction depends directly on the relation existing between the genetic constitution of the zygote producing the female gamete and the genetic constitution of the male gamete. *cf* Zygotic Incompatibility (*cf.* MATHER).

Gametic Lethal Factor. — A gene which renders inviable a gamete which carries it.

Gametic Mutation. — A mutation occurring during gamete formation.

Gametic Number. — The number of chromosomes in the nuclei of gametes.

Gametic Reduction. — Meiosis which takes place immediately prior to fertilization.

Gametic Sterility. — Sterility due to the production of degenerate non-functional gametes, haplontic sterility

Gametocyte. — A gamete mother-cell, or gametogonium.

Gametogenesis. — The formation of gametes.

Gametogenic. — Arising from spontaneous changes in chromosomes of gametes (HENDERSON).

Gametogonium. — A gametocyte or gamete mother-cell.

Gametophyte. — The haplont or haploid plant from which the gametes arise in types showing an alternation of generations.

Gamic. — Fertilized.

Gamobium. — The sexual generation where there is an alternation of generations.

Gamogenesis. — Reproduction by sexual fertilization.

Gamogenic. — Arising as a result of sexual fertilization.

Gamogony. — Reproduction by means of special **sexually**-differentiated cells (gametes).

Gamont. — Gametocyte, *q.v.*

Gamopetalous. — Having the petals united.

Gamophase. — The gametic phase of the life cycle; the haploid portion of the life cycle.

Gamosepalous. — Having the sepals joined.

Gamotropism. — Mutual attraction as between gametes.

Geitonogamy. — Self-pollination in which the pollen is derived from another flower on the same plant.

Geitonogenesis. — Similarity of appearance acquired independently and at about the same time by unrelated forms. Adj. **Geitonogenetic.** *cf.* Hypogenesis.

Gemmation. — The production of specialized buds which are capable of developing into a new independent organism.

Gemmule. — Pangen, *q.v.*

Genasthenia, Theory of. — In addition to their accepted qualitative properties, this theory attributes to the genes quantitative characteristics, or functional valency, which may be reduced in a heterozygote or in a partly foreign plasma.

Gene. — The unit of inheritance, which occupies a fixed chromosomal locus, is transmitted in the germ cells, and which governs, affects or controls the transmission and development of a hereditary character.

Gene Base. — *See* Protosome.

Gene Centres. — *See* under Protosome.

Gene Complex. — The balanced system of genes which constitutes the 'internal environment' within which each gene must act. The system is so balanced that the alteration of any one gene affects the operation of many others (FORD).
The genetic background of a particular gene, comprising all the genes which in any way react on, modify or affect the character controlled by the gene in question.

Gene-flow. — The spread of genes which takes place within a group (variety, subspecies, or species) as a result of outcrossing followed by natural crossing within the group.

Gene Interaction. — The action of non-allelic genes upon each other.

Gene-locus. — Used by some as synonymous with gene and by others to mean locus, *q.v.*

Gene Mutation. — A heritable variation due to an alteration at a definite locus on a chromosome.

Gene Starvation, Theory of. — A theory put forward by THOMPSON (1938) suggesting that to reproduce itself normally a gene must have available in its vicinity all the necessary 'parts' Lack of any 'part' during the stage between successive nuclear divisions is suggested as the cause of mutation, or alternatively of gene deficiency, at the 'starved' locus On this theory, differential nutrition in the early stages of segmentation of the fertilized ovum gives rise to mass mutation in certain groups of cells from which are produced the primordia of the differentiated adult tissues

Gene String — The central chromosome thread on which the genes are, assumedly, arranged in sequence

Gene Substitution. — The replacement of one gene by its allele, all the other genes (or all other relevant genes) remaining unchanged

Genecology. — (i) A combination of genetics and ecology, the study of the interactions of environment and genetic constitution (ii) Ecology which is mainly concerned with species.

Genepistasis. — The concept that evolution may often long remain at a standstill at a definite stage.

Generational Sterility. — Basic, inherent sterility due to such causes as an unbalanced chromosome number, or lack of homology as between the two chromosome sets in an interspecific hybrid, as opposed to sterility due to malformed anthers or pollen incompatibility

Generative Apogamy. — Reduced apogamy, haploid parthenogenesis. *See* under Parthenogenesis

Generative Apospory. — The formation of gametophytes from archesporial cells or their derivatives which lack the character of spores (FAGERLIND).

Generative Nucleus. — The gametic nucleus of a pollen grain as distinct from the vegetative or tube-nucleus

Generitype. — The type species of a genus

Genetic Complex. — A collective term for all the hereditary factors borne in an organism

Genetic Factor. — Gene, *q v*

Genetic Isolation — Separation of groups by the formation of inter-group sterility barriers

Genetic Polymorphism. —— The co-existence of two or more genetically-determined and well defined forms ("phases") of a species in the same area (HUXLEY)

Genetic Variation. — A heritable variation produced by a change in the genes, *e g*. a mutation, deletion, recombination, etc.

Genetics. — Genetics is the science which seeks to account for the resemblances and differences which are exhibited by organisms related by descent (BABCOCK & CLAUSEN).

Genetype. — Genotype, *q.v.*

Genic Balance. — A state of harmonious adjustment of the interaction of the genes of an organism so that its development is normal. The concept that an individual gene does not act solely by reason of its inherent qualities but by reason of its interaction with other genes in the gene-complex.

Genitals. — The external reproductive organs

Genocline. — A geographical gradient in genetic composition (usually due to gene-flow).

Genome, Genom. — A chromosome set, *i.e.* the chromosome complement of a gamete.

Genomere — A hypothetical subdivision of a gene.

Genome-mutation. — An alteration involving one or more complete sets of chromosomes as in polyploidy (including autopolyploidy and allopolyploidy), or involving one or more approximately complete sets of chromosomes as in aneuploidy.

Genonema-ta. — The protein frame-work of a chromonema

Genonomy. — The study of the familial relationships of the individuals which comprise a species (EPLING).

Genorheithrum — The stream of genes passing down a phylogenetic stock (CAIN, 1944).

Genosome. — The physical part of a chromosome at the point where a gene is located.

Genospecies. — A group, all the members of which are genotypically identical.

Genotype. — The entire genetic constitution, expressed and latent, of an organism. The term can also be used in dealing with the genetic constitution of an individual with respect to any limited number of genes under examination. A group of organisms all with the same factorial constitution.

Genotypes, Number of. — The number of distinct genotypes expected in F_2 is given by calculating 3^n where n is the number of factor-pairs involved. In a backcross the number of genotypes is 2^n.

Genotypic. — Pertaining to the genotype; controlled by the genotype.

Genotypic Control. — The genetic control of the activities of chromosomes especially with regard to nuclear division.

Genovariation. — A heritable change taking place at a single gene locus, presumably caused by chemical alteration of the

individual gene; a mutation proper, transgenation or point
mutation.

Genuine Pleiotropism. — The controlling, by a single gene,
of "two (or more) different effects which it produces directly
and by the use of *different* mechanisms. *Spurious pleiotropism*
may be brought about in two ways. Either the gene does two
(or more) things *directly*, but by means of the *same* mechanism, or else it has one effect which in turn causes other things
to happen" (GRUNEBERG)

Geoclines. — The graduations of variation produced within a
species by adaptation within an area showing geographical
variation extending over considerable distances

Geographical Divergence. — The evolution from a single
ancestral form of two or more different forms, subspecies, or
species, each in a different geographical area.

Geographical Race. — "A complex of interbreeding and completely fertile individuals which are morphologically identical
or vary only within the limits of individual ecological and seasonal variability The typical characters of this group of individuals are genetically fixed and no other geographical race
of the same species occurs within the same range" (RENSCH,
quoted by MAYR, 1942).

Geographic Speciation. — The gradual formation of new
species by reason of the spatial isolation of different stocks
of the original species

Geratology. — The study or science dealing with senescence
and decadence.

Germ Cells. — Gametes, or cells which give rise to gametes.

Germen. — The reproductive glands.

Germinal Selection. — Selective competition as between
gametes.

Germinal Spot. — The nucleolus of an unfertilized egg

Germinal Vesicle. — The nucleus of a primary oocyte.

Germplasm. — The material basis of heredity. WEISMANN's
term for the hereditary substance in the germ-cells; idioplasm.

Gerontic. — Appertaining to senescence or decadence.

Gerontomorphosis. — Evolution which is brought about by
variations affecting adult organisms and which is characterized
by increasing specialization and a decreasing capacity for
further evolution. The production of phylogenetic effects by
the modification of characters which were already present in
the ancestral line of adults.

Gestation. — Pregnancy; the carrying of the foetus in the uterus, the period during which the foetus is carried in the uterus.

Gestation Periods. — Averages, in days:

Ass	369	Fox, silver	52
Ass, Somali	365	Goat	151
Ass x mare	353	Guinea-pig	66
Bison, American	273	Horse	337
Bison, European	276	Human	
Buffalo	310	fertilization-labour	269
Camel, bactrian	395	menstruation-labour	281
Camel, dromedary	336	Pig, domestic	114
Cat, domestic	57	Rabbit	31
Cattle, *Bos taurus*	283	Rat	22
Cattle, *B indicus*	286	Rhesus Monkey	165
Dog	62	Sheep, domestic	148
Elephant, African	641	Sheep, barbary	160
Elephant, Indian	626	Sheep, bighorn	180
Ferret	42		

Gigantism. — Appearance of giant forms (often polyploid).

Glandular Hermaphroditism. — The presence in the one gonad of both ovarian and testicular material.

Gliding Intergradation. — Continuous variation.

Gloger's Rule. — The melanins increase in the warm and humid parts of the range. Reddish or yellowish-brown phaeomelanins prevail in arid climates where the blackish eumelanins are reduced. The phaeomelanins are subject to reduction in cold climate, and in extreme cases also the eumelanins (polar white) (MAYR, 1942).

Golgi Apparatus. — A mechanism, found almost exclusively in animal cells, which moves about in the immediate vicinity of the nucleus and consists either of minute structures, called Golgi bodies, or a single reticulate mechanism.

Golgi Nets. — A part of the Golgi element.

Gonad. — An organ within which ova or spermatozoa are formed.

Gonadectomy. — Excision of gonads.

Gonadotrophic, Gonadotropic Hormones. — Any hormones which stimulate the gonad.

Gonadotrophin. — A general term for any gonadotrophic hormone, *i.e.* a hormone which stimulates the gonads. Gonadotrophin (A.P.) is a preparation made from anterior pituitaries,

—— (M.S) is obtained from the urine of pregnant mares, and —— (P.U.) is obtained from the urine of pregnant women.

Goneoclin — Of heterozygotes: closely resembling one parent due to dominance.

Gones. — The four cells, or their nuclei, which are normally the immediate product of meiosis.

Gonia. — A general name for oogonia and spermatogonia.

Gonidangium. — An organ producing gonia

Gonidia. — (sing **Gonidium**). Gonia, *q v.*

Gonoblast. — A reproductive cell in animals.

Gonochorism. — Sex determination in animals.

Gonochoristic. — Of animals, having separate sexes.

Gonocyte. — A cell which gives rise to gametes.

Gonogenesis. — The process leading to the formation of gametes.

Gonomery. — The state of having the maternal and paternal genomes remaining more or less independent after the fusion of the male and female pronuclei.

Gonoplasm — Reproductive protoplasm

Gonosomic Mosaic. — An individual whose gonads carry a lethal gene in every cell but whose somatic cells do not all carry this lethal.

Gonotokont. — Auxocyte, *q v.*

Graafian Follicle. — A vesicle which in mammals, surrounds the ovum

Grade. — An individual only one of whose parents (typically the sire) is a purebred.

Grading. — The mating of a scrub animal, or of a grade animal, to a purebred animal (usually the sire).

Graft. — An artificially induced vegetative fusion or union of parts from different individuals, the rooted part is called the stock and the part, or parts, inserted or otherwise vegetatively fused to it, the scion(s)

Graft Chimaera. — *See* Graft Hybrid.

Graft Hybrid. — A plant made up of two genetically distinct types of tissue, due to fusion after grafting; graft chimaera.

Gravid. — Of a uterus: pregnant.

Group Variation. — Variation between different populations within a species, as distinct from "individual variation" which is the variation *within* a population.

Gynaecium, Gynoecium, Gynoeceum. — The carpels or pistils in a flower.

Gynaeocentric Theory. — The concept placing the more important role of evolution on the female sex of plants (CARPENTER)

Gynaecomorph. — A male individual which in appearance resembles a female

Gynander. — *See* Gynandromorph.

Gynandromorph. — A sexual chimaera, often male on one side and female on the other (bilateral gynander). *See* Gynergate, Ergatomorphic Male and Dinergatandromorph.

Gynecogenic. — Parthenogenetic

Gynecomast. — A male with female type of mammary development

Gynergate. — A 'female-worker' type of sex-mosaic which occurs in ants **Lateral** ———. An individual, one side of which shows female characteristics and the other side 'worker' characters

Gynodioecious. — Dioecious, with some flowers hermaphrodite, others pistillate only, on separate plants (JACKSON).

Gynoecium. — Gynaecium, *q v.*

Gynogenesis. — Pseudo-fertilization in which the male gamete, though it penetrates the ovum does not fertilize it so that further development is parthenogenetic.

Gynomonoecious. — Having pistillate and perfect flowers on the one plant.

Haeckel's Law. — Biogenetic law, *q v.*

Haldane's Law. — When in the first generation between hybrids between two species, one sex is absent, rare, or sterile, that sex is always the heterogametic sex

Half Race. — A "race" of plants whose phenotypic characteristics are the result of the heterozygosity of certain genes. Such a "race" can never breed true but always produces a proportion of plants typical of the "race" in each generation.

Half-spindle. — A uni-polar type of spindle occurring during meiosis in some insects

Half Spindle Components. — Chromosomal fibres, *q v.*

Haplo-. — The term haplo-, followed by a symbol designating a particular chromosome, indicates an individual in whose somatic cells one member of this particular chromosome-pair is lacking. Thus, in *Drosophila,* Haplo-IV means a fly in which one member of the chromosome IV pair is missing. *cf.* Diplo- and Triplo-.

Haplobiont. — A plant in which there is no alternation of generations so that there is only one type of individual in the complete life-history.

Haplochlamydeous Chimaera. — A chimaera in which the epidermis forms one component and the inner tissues the other. *cf.* Dichlamidius.

Haplo-Diploid System. — A sex system in which one sex is haploid and the other diploid.

Haplodiplont. — A haploid spore-producing plant

Haploid. — Single, having the reduced number of chromosomes typical of gametes as opposed to the somatic number. *See* Diploid Set of Chromosomes.

Haploid Apogamety, Haploid Apogamy. — Reduced apogamy, haploid parthenogenesis. *See* under Parthenogenesis.

Haploid Incompatibility. — Homomorphic incompatibility (*q.v*) as between haploid individuals (as in the Fungi) in which the diploid phase does not enter into the incompatibility reaction.

Haploid-insufficient. — Used of duplicate genes to indicate that neither of them will, in the heterozygous state, give full expression to the character, incompletely dominant

Haploid Parthenogenesis. — *See* under Parthenogenesis.

Haploid-sufficient. — Used of duplicate genes to indicate that either of them, in the heterozygous state, gives full expression to the character, completely dominant

Haplomict. — A hybrid carrying a single genom made up of chromosomes and portions of chromosomes from different sources (Occurs in certain algae and bryophytes)

Haplomitosis. — Type of cell division where nuclear granules form chromospires which withdraw in two groups or divide transversely in the middle (HENDERSON).

Haplont. — A plant in which fertilization is followed immediately by a reduction division so that all nuclei, other than the zygotic nucleus, are haploid, *e g*. most fungi and algae.

Haplontic Sterility. — Sterility due to the production of degenerate non-functional gametes, gametic sterility.

Haplophase. — The stage in the life-cycle of an organism when the nuclei contain the haploid number of chromosomes.

Haplosis. — The halving of the somatic chromosome number at meiosis.

Haplostemonous. — Possessing only one whorl of stamens

Haplozygous. — Hemizygous, *q.v.*

Hardy's Formula. — If AA and aa individuals are mixed in the proportion of q and 1-q respectively, then in a population in which random mating is the rule, the population in all subsequent generations will consist of. q^2AA . $2q (1-q) Aa$: $(1-q)^2 aa$.

Heat. — The period of sexual excitement in female animals during the breeding season

Hemeranthic. — Flowering by day.

Hemikaryon. — A haploid nucleus.

Hemikaryotic. — With half the somatic number of chromosomes, haploid.

Hemizygous. — Of a gene: present in the unpaired state, as in haploid organisms, or in an unpaired sex chromosome, or in a differential segment of a sex chromosome.

Hercogamy. — The state of being incapable of self-fertilization owing to the position of the stamens in relation to the stigma or stigmas.

Hereditary. — (i) In the clinical sense: transmitted with unbroken continuity from generation to generation (ii) In the genetic sense. controlled by a genetic mechanism which is

capable of being transmitted from generation to generation
although the outward signs of the presence of this mechanism
may only be apparent under specific conditions

Hereditary Univalents — Chromosomes which have evolved
a system of more or less even distribution in segregation without going through the process of pachytene pairing. *cf.* Spontaneous Univalent

Heredity. — The transmission of parental qualities, expressed
or latent, to the progeny.

Heritability. — The portion of the observed variance for
which differences in heredity are responsible

Herkogamy. — *See* Hercogamy.

Hermaphrodite. — In plants, monoclinous or monoecious;
having the organs of both sexes in one individual.

Hermaphroditism. — The condition in which the reproductive
organs of both sexes are present in one individual.

Heterauxesis. — The relation of the growth-rate of a part
of a developing organism (whether morphological or chemical)
to the growth-rate of the whole or of another part, a comparison between organisms of the same group but of different
ages and hence sizes (HUXLEY, NEEDHAM and LERNER).

Heteroauxin. — B-indolylacetic acid, a plant growth stimulant
present in urine.

Heteroauxone. — Any substance which is biologically highly
active but which the organism does not, itself, synthesize.

Heterobrachial Chromosome. — A chromosome which is
divided into two unequal segments by the centromere

Heterocarpous. — Producing more than one kind of fruit.

Heterocaryon, Heterokaryon. — An individual whose cells
are heterokaryotic.

Heterocaryosis. — Heterokaryosis, *q.v.*

Heterocephalous — With staminate and pistillate flowers
on separate heads on the same plant.

Heterochlamydeous. — Having the perianth clearly divided
into a calyx and a corolla.

Heterochromatic. — Of a chromosome, or portion of a chromosome staining deeply (and presumed to consist of genetically
inert material). *cf.* Euchromatic.

Heterochromatin. — Deeply staining chromatin presumed to
be genetically inert, as opposed to euchromatin which is genetically active and stains less deeply Heterochromatin remains
condensed and stainable during interphase. The heterochromatin possibly contains the polygenes.

Heterochromatism. — Appearance of different colours in the flowers of the same infloresence due to seasonal differences (CARPENTER).

Heterochromaty. — Differential staining

Heterochromosomes. — Chromosomes distinguished by special peculiarities of behaviour, form, or size in contradistinction to autosomes or euchromosomes (MONTGOMERY, WILSON)

Heterochrony. — A reversal in the sequence of developmental stages during evolution.

Heteroclinous. — Heterocephalous, *q v.*

Heterofertilization — The process responsible for the production of seed in which embryo and endosperm differ genetically, generally as a result of 'fertilization' by two unlike pollen grains, the sperm from one of which fertilizes the egg cell whilst the generative nucleus of the other unites with the two polar nuclei.

Heterogameon. — A species made up of races which, if selfed, produce morphologically stable populations, but when crossed may produce several types of viable and fertile offspring (CAMP & GILLY).

Heterogamete. — A gamete differing in its properties of sex determination, or morphologically, from the other conjugant; anisogamete.

Heterogametic. — Producing gametes of more than one kind, which differ in regard to their properties of sex determination or in the chromosomes which they contain. Opp. Homogametic.

Heterogametic Sex. — The sex which has two dissimilar sex chromosomes in its body cells (*e.g.* the human male)

Heterogamety. — The production of gametes having different properties of sex determination

Heterogamous. — (1) Bearing two or more kinds of flowers on the one inflorescence, often a unisexual peripheral group and a perfect central group as in *Compositae*. (11) Heterogametic, *q.v.*

Heterogamy. — The condition of having gametes which are dissimilar especially in regard to their properties of sex determination.

Heterogenesis. — (1) Alternation of generations, an alternation of a sexual with an asexual form or, cytologically, the alternation of a haploid with a diploid stage (11) The appearance of a new distinct form differing from its parents and capable of transmitting its distinctive traits to its offspring. (iii) The derivation of a living thing from something unlike itself

Heterogenetic Association. — The pairing, in an allotetraploid, of chromosomes derived from different ancestral stocks.

Heterogenetic Pairing. — Pairing and subsequent segregation between chromosomes derived from the two parental species of an allopolyploid.

Heterogonic Growth. — The growth of two parts, or organs, at different rates which, however, keep a constant ratio to each other

Heterogony. — (i) Reproduction by parthenogenesis as well as by sexual means. (ii) The state of having heterogonic growth

Heterogynism. — Having the female of a species showing a more marked geographic variation than the male.

Heterokaryosis. — The presence of genetically different nuclei within individual cells of a mycelium (E. Sansome).

Heterokaryotic Vigour. — Increased vigour comparable with hybrid vigour but due to the presence together of two or more genetically different types of nuclei in the mycelial cells.

Heterokinesis. — The meiotic division during which gametes of different sex-potentiality become separated by differential distribution of the sex chromosomes.

Heterolecithal. — Off eggs: having the yolk unevenly distributed

Heteromorphic. — Used of chromosome pairs the two members of which differ in size or in shape.

Heteromorphic Incompatibility. — Incompatibility (q v.) which is associated with, and dependent on, variation in floral morphology (MATHER).

Heteromorphosis. — The production of an organ at a place other than that in which it belongs, homoosis.

Heteromorphous. — (i) Atypical. (ii) Bearing two or more kinds of flower on the one plant (iii) Having more than one form.

Heterophytic. — Dioecious, q v.

Heteroplastic Graft. — A graft, or transplantation of tissue, between different species or between different genera as opposed to a homeoplastic graft, q v. See Xenoplastic Graft.

Heteroploid. — Having a chromosome number which is not an exact multiple of the basic haploid number; an individual whose nuclei are of this type.

Heteropolar. — Of pairing chromosomes: having the attraction force unevenly distributed throughout the length of the chromosome (as at pachytene).

Heteropycnosis. — Differential contraction or condensation of a sex chromosome vis a vis the autosomes. This property is called **Negative Heteropycnosis** when condensation is slower in the sex chromosome than in the others and **Positive Heteropycnosis** when the sex chromosome shows precocious condensation as compared with the other chromosomes. The property of heteropycnosis is not entirely limited to the sex chromosomes

Heteropycnotic Chromosome. — A chromosome which has thickened (condensed) to a greater or less extent than the remainder of the chromosome complement

Heterosomes. — The sex chromosomes. See Heterochromosomes.

Heterosis — (1) The increased vigour often exhibited by hybrid individuals. (ii) The state of being formed from the union of gametes of dissimilar genetic constitution, heterozygosis. Adj. **Heterotic.**

Heterostylous. — (1) Differentiated into long- and short-styled plants (ii) Bearing two, or more, kinds of flowers on the one inflorescence, generally a peripheral strap-like group of neuter or male flowers and an inner group of hermaphrodite flowers as in *Compositae*, heterostyled; heterogamous

Heterostyly. — Differentiation into long- and short-styled plants.

Heterosynapsis. — Pairing between unlike chromosomes. *cf.* Homosynapsis.

Heterotetraploid. — (i) Having four complete sets of chromosomes plus one or more additional chromosomes. (ii) An organism whose somatic nuclei are of this type

Heterothally. — Genetically controlled incompatibility in fungi.

Heterotic Vigour. — Hybrid vigour.

Heterotropic Chromosome. — A sex chromosome; a chromosome which has no truly similar homologue in the heterozygous sex. *See* W-, X- and Y-Chromosomes.

Heterotype, or Heterotypic, Division. — The first division in meiosis.

Heterozygosis. — The state of being formed from the union of gametes of dissimilar genetic constitution.

Heterozygote. — An organism derived from the union of gametes of dissimilar genetic constitution.

Heterozygote, Complex. — A heterozygote whose gametes have numerous differences which segregate as a unit (RENNER; DARLINGTON).

Heterozygotes, Proportion of. — In a population mating at random, the proportion of individuals heterozygous for any particular gene can be found from the equation $p^2 : 2pq\ q^2$ where p^2 and q^2 are the proportions of the two homozygous classes respectively, $2pq$ represents the proportion of heterozygotes, and $p + q = 1$

Heterozygous. — Derived from the union of gametes of dissimilar genetic constitution.

Heterozygous Sex. — That sex in which the sex chromosomes are dissimilar or in which the sex chromosome has no homologue. Gametes produced by the heterozygous sex are of two kinds with regard to their properties of sex determination. *See* Y-chromosomes and W-chromosomes

Hexad. — Unequal bivalent (not trivalent) formed by pairing of one chromosome with its homologue which has fused with a third non-homologous chromosome, in a fusion heterozygote (McCLUNG, DARLINGTON).

Hexaploid. — Having six haploid sets of chromosomes in the somatic cells.

Hexoestrol. — This synthetic oestrogen is more active than either oestrone or stilboestrol *See* under Oestrogens.

Hexuronic Acid. — Ascorbic Acid, vitamin C, $C_6H_8O_6$, a water-soluble anti-scorbutic vitamin

Hinny. — The offspring of a stallion and a she-ass

Histogenesis. — The formation or differentiation of specialised tissues.

Hofacker & Sadler Law. — The theory that sex determination is affected by the relative ages of the male and female parents. An older male parent was supposed to give a predisposition to male offspring and a male parent younger than the female was thought to produce a higher proportion of females in the offspring.

Holandric. — Of a character. passing direct from male to male through the Y-chromosome.

Hologametes. — Gametes which are of similar size to typical cells of the species, and which are not formed by meiosis.

Hologamy. — Having gametes which are not formed by meiosis and which resemble the ordinary somatic cells of the organism; the fusion of such gametes

Hologenic. — Of a sex-linked character passing direct from female to female.

Holotype. — A single specimen selected from the cotypes (q v) and designated the type

Homeokinesis — Normal mitosis in which the daughter nuclei each receive a similar and equal chromosome complement.

Homeologous Chromosomes. — *See* Homoeologous Chromosomes.

Homeologue. — A homoeologous chromosome, q v.

Homeoplastic Graft — A tissue graft made between individuals of the same species cf Heteroplastic Graft and Xenoplastic Graft.

Homeosynapsis. — Homosynapsis, the pairing of homologous chromosomes

Homeotypic Division. — The second meiotic division.

Homoeologous Chromosomes — Chromosomes that are homologous in parts of their length (HUSKINS, 1941).

Homoeologue. — A homoeologous chromosome, q.v.

Homoeosis. —— Homoosis, q v.

Homogametes — Gametes which are alike in their properties of sex determination.

Homogametic. — Producing gametes with identical properties of sex determination and which are all alike as to the chromosomes which they contain Opp Heterogametic

Homogametic Sex. — The homozygous sex; that sex which produces gametes of only one kind with regard to their properties of sex determination. *See* X- and Y-chromosomes.

Homogamy. — (i) The condition of simultaneous ripening of anthers and stigmas in a flower (ii) Inbreeding caused by spatial isolation (iii) The tendency of like to mate with like. Adj. Homogamous. cf Dichogamy

Homogeneon. — A species which is genetically and morphologically homogeneous, all members being interfertile (CAMP & GILLY).

Homogenetic Pairing or Association. — Pairing between truly homologous chromosomes, particularly used in allopolyploids, of pairing between chromosomes derived from one of the parental species.

Homogeny. — Similarity as between parts of different organisms due to common ancestry. Adj. Homogenous.

Homogony. — Having the pistils and stamens of all flowers of uniform relative length

Homolecithal. — Of eggs: having equally distributed yolk.

Homologous Chromosomes. — Chromosomes in which the same gene loci occur in the same sequence.

Homology. — Similarity of structures due to similarity of origin. N. **Homologue.** Adj. **Homologous.**

Homology, Residual. — A degree of affinity still existing between once truly homologous chromosomes, which will now only rarely permit crossing-over between them (STEPHENS). *cf.* Homoeologous Chromosomes.

Homomorphic. — Of chromosome pairs: morphologically indistinguishable. Opp. Heteromorphic.

Homomorphic Incompatibility. — Incompatibility (*q.v*) which is not dependent for its action on morphological variation.

Homonculus, Homunculus. — The miniature foetus erroneously thought to be present in a human spermatozoon.

Homoosis. — The production in one particular region of an individual, of an appendage normally occurring in a different region of the individual's body.

Homophytic. — Monoecious, *q.v.*

Homoplasy. — Similarity due to adaptation to common functions or similar environments. Adj **Homoplastic.**

Homopolar. — Of pairing chromosomes: having the attraction force evenly distributed throughout the length of the chromosome (as at zygotene).

Homosynapsis. — Pairing of homologous chromosomes. *cf.* Heterosynapsis.

Homotype Division. — Homotypic Division, *q v.*

Homotypic Division. — The second, or non-reductional, meiotic division.

Homozygosis. — The state of having any specific gene(s) in the double condition so that the organism is pure-breeding for that (or those) particular gene(s) since all its gametes contain it (or them).

Homozygosis Frequency. — The frequency with which one allele of a heterozygous gene-pair becomes homozygous in the succeeding generation, the gene-pair concerned being situated in attached X-chromosomes

Homozygote. — An organism having any specified gene, or genes homozygous. *See* Homozygosis and Homozygous.

Homozygotes, Proportion of. — *See* Appendix 1.

Homozygotization. — The rendering of a species, group, etc. homozygous.

Homozygous. — Of an organism: having any specified gene or genes, present in the double condition (AA as distinct from Aa) *See* Homozygosis.

Homozygous Sex. — The homogametic sex; that sex which produces gametes of only one kind with regard to their properties of sex determination. *See* X- and Y-chromosomes.

Hormone. — A hormone is a product of animal metabolism, effective in very small amounts, produced by special endocrine glands and active on the organism itself in a very specific manner (SCHOPFER).

Horotelic. — Evolving at a certain modal rate, as opposed to Bradytelic (evolving considerably slower than the modal rate) and Tachytelic (evolving much faster than the modal rate).

Hyaloplasm. — The clear, non-granular protoplasm of a cell in which the cytomicrosomes are suspended.

Hybrid. — The product of a cross between individuals of unlike genetic constitution. *See*, also, Numerical — and Structural —.

Hybrid Cline. — Northocline; an extension of the term cline (*q v.*) to cover the gradation of forms which occurs in nature following inter-specific hybridization

Hybrid Swarm. — A hybrid population typically occurring in the overlapping area between inter-fertile species or subspecies.

Hybrid Vigour. — The increased vigour often exhibited by hybrid individuals; heterosis.

Hybridism. — The state of being hybrid.

Hybridization. — The crossing of individuals of unlike genetic constitution. *See* Allopatric — and Sympatric —.

Hybridization, Introgressive. — Hybridization in which infiltration of the germplasm of one species into another occurs; typically such infiltration is brought about by chance back-crossing.

Hybridogenous Pseudo-parthenogenesis. — Seed production following stimulation by pollen the male nucleus of which becomes eliminated before fertilization so that a maternal embryo is formed which, as a result of doubling, is diploid (In some of these cases it has been shown that the endosperm is of hybrid origin although the embryo is purely maternal).

Hydrophilous. — Water-pollinated.

Hydroxyprogesterone. — A hormone secreted by the corpus luteum in the ovary and controlling events in pregnancy (MOTTRAM, 1944)

Hygroplasm. — The more liquid portion of protoplasm.

Hyperchimaera. — A chimaera whose components are not arranged in sectors but are agglomerated to form a mosaic.

Hyperchromasy. — Of a cell· possessing an abnormally high proportion of chromatin before division

Hyperchromatosis. — Hyperchromasy, *q v*

Hypercyesis. — Fertilization of a second ovum in a pregnant animal after a considerable interval from the original conception.

Hyperdiploidy. — The state of having a translocated portion of a chromosome present in addition to the normal complement; sectional hyperploidy

Hypermorphosis. — This occurs when an animal, in the course of its own ontogeny, passes through the ontogenetic stages of its ancestors but develops beyond the final adult stage of its ancestors; overstepping.

Hyperploid — (1) A heteroploid in which the chromosome number is slightly greater than the nearest multiple of the haploid number. (11) Having a chromosome number slightly in excess of the nearest multiple of the basic number. *See* also Sectional Hyperploidy and Hyperdiploidy.

Hypertely. — (i) The evolution of unduly large individuals, or parts of individuals. (ii) Mimetic adaptation which has passed beyond close resemblance

Hyphal Aversion. — A form of incompatibility, in fungi, in which the hyphae of incompatible strains cease growing or reverse their direction of growth whenever they approach to within a few millimetres of each other.

Hypnosis — The dormancy of seeds.

Hypogenesis. — (i) Asexual development (11) Similarity of appearance (or function) acquired independently, but at different periods, by unrelated forms. Adj **Hypogenetic,** *cf.* Geitonogenesis

Hypomorphic (Mutation). — A gene mutation producing an effect similar to but not so great as, that produced by a gene loss (deletion) (J. Heredity).

Hypophysectomise. — To excise the pituitary gland.

Hypophysectomy. — Excision of the pituitary gland.

Hypophysis. — The pituitary, a ductless gland situated at the base of the brain. The anterior lobe of the pituitary secretes a hormone which (*a*) governs, in the female, follicular maturation, ovulation and the formation of luteal tissue, and, in the male, the development of the testes and spermatogenesis, and (*b*) controls the production of hormones by the gonads.

Hypoploid. — Lacking one chromosome of the complement. *See* Haplo-.

Hypostasis. — Non-allelomorphic recessiveness *See* Epistasis.

Hypostatic. — Recessive (of non-allelomorphs). *See* Epistatic.

Hysteresis. — A lag in the movement at one level of integration in response to stress at another level, *e.g.*, in the adjustment of the external form of a chromosome to its internal stresses during the spiralisation cycle (DARLINGTON).

Hysterotely. — A condition, sometimes found in certain moths, in which the reproductive glands are segmentally repeated.

I_1, I_2, I_3. — First, second and third generations of self-fertilization.

Iarovization. — Vernalization, *q v.*

Id. — WEISMANN's term for a hereditary unit "necessary to the production of a complete individual".

Idant. — An obsolete synonym for chromosome, *q.v.*

Identical Twins. — Monozygotic twins, *i e* both originating from the one fertilized ovum

Idio-adaptation — Evolutionary changes which bring about specialization and a progressive restriction of the mode of life of the organism.

Idiochromatin. — Nuclear chromatin controlling cell division but otherwise dormant.

Idiochromidia. — Chromidia having a reproductive function and derived from idiochromatin.

Idiochromosome. — A sex chromosome; a chromosome which has no truly similar homologue in the heterozygous sex. *See* also under W-, X- and Y-chromosomes.

Idiogram. — A diagrammatic representation of the chromosome complement of a karyotype.

Idioplasm. — The generative portion of a cell as distinct from the vegetative, or nutritive, portion. NAGELI's term for the hereditary substance passed on from one generation to another; germplasm; chromatin.

Idiosome. — Idiozome, *q.v.*

Idiotype. — The individual genotype.

Idiovariation. — A mutation.

Idiozome. — The zone of non-granular protoplasm around the centrosome; the attraction sphere.

Illegitimate Pollination. — Artificial self-pollination of a flower which is specialized for cross-pollination.

Imaginal Tissue. — Undifferentiated tissue in the larva or embryo from which the external organs of the final instar (the imago or fully adult insect) develop. Specifically such tissues are called **Imaginal buds,** —— **discs,** —— **disks.**

Immunity. — Complete resistance to any particular disease or pest

Imperfect Arrhenogenic. — An individual which produces broods in which males predominate, only a small proportion of females being present.

Imperfect Flower — One which is not functionally (or anatomically) hermaphroditic

Implant. — A grafted portion of tissue

Impregnation. — The deposition of spermatozoa within the body of the female whether brought about by coitus or artificially, insemination.

Inantherate. — Lacking anthers.

Inarching. — The grafting of a branch of one plant onto another plant without cutting the branch away from the parent plant until union is complete.

Inbred Line. — A line showing a considerable degree of homozygosity as a result of continued inbreeding and selection.

Inbred-variety Cross. — The F_1 produced by crossing an inbred line and a commercial variety.

Inbreeding. — Breeding between close relatives, especially when repeated for several generations; endogamy.

Inbreeding Coefficient — *See* Appendix 1.

Incasement. — Preformation *See* under Epigenesis

Incompatibility. — The inability of pollen to bring about fertilization because the pollen-tubes are arrested in the style and prevented from reaching the ovules

Incomplete Penetrance. — Said of a gene which, though normally dominant or partially dominant, sometimes fails to produce an effect on a heterozygote, also of a recessive gene which does not always have any effect in the homozygous state. *See* also Penetrance and Complete Penetrance.

Independent Assortment. — The segregation of genes in gamete formation without any particular genes occurring together more frequently than would be expected on a chance basis

Independent Characters. — Characters governed by genes showing independent assortment, *q v.*

Independent Genes. — Genes which show independent assortment, *q v.*

Index-breeding. — A system of breeding in which the value of each sire is computed as a numerical 'index' from the relation of daughter's productive ability to that of their dams.

Indole-3-acetic Acid. — A plant growth hormone which has been used successfully in inducing polyploidy.

Induction, Somatic. — The transmission to the offspring of the effects of use and disuse.

Industrial Melanism. — The darkening of a population due to the selective effect of the darkened surroundings of an industrial area

Inert Chromosome. — A chromosome which appears to have few or no physiologically active genes.

Infundibulum. — The fimbriated, funnel-shaped portion of the oviduct immediately adjacent to the ovary.

Inhibiting Factors — Inhibitors, *q.v.*

Inhibitors. — Genes which show a special form of epistasis such that one gene renders another non-allelic gene entirely inoperative.

Initial Meiosis. — Meiosis which takes place in the first two divisions after fertilization, at the beginning of the life cycle of an organism; zygotic meiosis.

Initial Spindle. — A miniature spindle-like structure seen in the centrosome when the centriole divides, netrum.

Innate. — In-born, inherited.

Inositol. — A component of the vitamin B_2 complex.

Insertional Translocation. — The inclusion of a fragment of one chromosome in a non-homologous chromosome in a non-terminal position

Insertion Region. — The centromere, spindle attachment or kinetochore; a non-staining localized region in each chromosome to which the spindle 'fibre' appears to be attached at metaphase. The centromere remains single for some time after the rest of the chromosome has divided and at anaphase, starts to move towards the pole before the rest of the chromatid.

Instaminate. — Lacking stamens.

Instantaneous Sympatric Speciation. — *See* Sympatric Speciation, Instantaneous.

Intelligence Quotient. — By intelligence tests an individual can be assigned to a "mental age" group (on the basis of the average marks obtained by a typical group of that age). This "mental age" divided by the actual age of the individual gives the "mental ratio" and this multiplied by 100 is the "intelligence quotient"

Intensifying Factors. — Modifying factors which increase the effect of a major gene

Interacting Mutations. — Mutations which give rise to complementary factors, *q v.*

Interaction Theory. — A theory of quantitative factor inheritance which assumes that the effect of each factor on the genotype is dependent upon all the other factors present, the visible effect of a certain factor being smaller the greater the number of factors acting in the same direction (RAMUSSON).

Intercalary Trabant. — *See* Trabant.

Interchange. — An exchange of segments between non-homologous chromosomes.

Interference. — The effect whereby one crossing-over lessens the probability of another occurring in its vicinity.

Interference Distance. — *See* under Differential and Interference Distances.

Inter-genic Changes. — Mutational changes involving more than one locus, *e.g.* inversions, deletions, translocations, duplications.

Intergradation. — This occurs where "two reasonably distinct units come into contact and gradually merge in the area under consideration". **Primary Intergradation** "exists if the steepening of the slope developed gradually and took place while all the populations involved were in continuous contact". **Secondary Intergradation** "refers to cases in which the two units, now connected by a steeply sloping character gradient, were separated completely at one time and have now come into contact again, after a number of differences have evolved" (MAYR, 1942).

Interkinesis. — *See* Interphase.

Intermediate. — A heterozygote whose phenotypic characters (or any specified character) are not identical with those of either parent but partake of the appearance of both.

Intermitosis. — The resting stage which often occurs between two mitotic divisions; interphase.

Interphase. — The resting phase in meiosis; the phase between the two meiotic divisions when the nucleus is at rest in the sense of not dividing; intermitosis; interkinesis.

Intersexes. — (i) Individuals intermediate between male and female but not functionally hermaproditic and differing from gynandromorphs in that they are not made up of a mixture of male and female sectors but are truly intermediate. (ii) A sexual abnormality in which the individual develops first as one sex and then the other. *See* Gynergate, Ergatomorphic Male, Dinergatandromorph, and Phenotypic Intersex.

Interspecific Selection. — Selection which operates to improve the competitive power of one species in relation to other species, as distinct from Intraspecific Selection, *q.v.*

Interzonal Fibres. — The spindle fibres which link the daughter chromosomes at anaphase and at the beginning of telophase.

Intra-genic Changes. — Mutational alterations in the nature of the individual gene, as opposed to inter-genic changes, *q v.*

Intra-nuclear Mitosis. — Mitotic nuclear division which takes place within the nuclear membrane without any cooperation from the cytoplasm

Intra-sexual Selection. — Competition as between the members of one sex, particularly competition as between males in reproduction.

Intraspecific Selection. — Selection which operates as between individuals within a species, as distinct from interspecific selection, *q v.*

Introgression. — Infiltration of the germplasm of one species into another; typically such infiltration would be brought about by chance backcrossing.

Introgressive Hybridization. — *See* Introgression.

Inversion — The reversal of one segment of a chromosome relative to the remainder and the consequent linear reversal of the gene sequence in the inverted segment relative to the rest of the chromosome

Inversion, Overlapping. — A compound inversion caused by a second inversion which includes part of a previously inverted segment.

Inversion Heterozygote. — A zygote in whose cells one or more of the chromosomes possess an inverted segment which is not inverted in the partners of these chromosomes, inversion hybrid; a form of structural hybrid.

Inversion Hybrid. — An inversion heterozygote, *q v.*

I.Q. — Intelligence Quotient, *q v.*

Irregular Dominance. — A form of dominance in which the gene shows variable expression in the heterozygous state, being on some genetic backgrounds coupled with certain environmental conditions, recessive, but showing, on other backgrounds, various degrees of dominance

Irreversibility, Dollo's Law of. — *See* under Dollo.

Isauxesis. — Ontogenetic heterauxesis in which the growth of the part is at the same rate as that of the body as a whole.

Iso-alleles. — Alleles which are indistinguishable except by special tests.

Iso-allely. — The state or condition of having isoalleles, *q v.*

Isochromatid Breaks. — 1-hit chromatid breaks, sister-reunions; aberrations which "involve breaks in both sister chromatids at the same locus (as far as can be seen), followed by lateral fusion to produce a dicentric chromatid and an acentric U-shaped fragment" (LEA & CATCHESIDE).

Iso-chromosome. — A chromosome with two identical arms, it is thought to be derived from a telocentric chromosome by the junction of sister chromatids.

Isogamete. — One of a pair of morphologically similar gametes.

Isogamous. — Having gametes which are undifferentiated, or morphologically similar. N. **Isogamy.**

Isogamy. — Union of morphologically similar gametes. Adj. Isogamous.

Isogenetic. — Of similar origin.

Isogenic. — (i) Homozygous. (ii) Apogamous. *See* Apogamy.

Isogenic Line. — A group, all the members of which have identical hereditary make-up (*e g.* clone, homozygous inbred line, identical twins).

Isogenomatic. — Of zygotic or somatic nuclei: composed of similar genoms.

Isogenous. — Of plants whose male and female gametes behave similarly in the transmission of inherited characters. N. **Isogeny.** *cf.* Anisogenous.

Isogeny. — *See* Isogenous.

Isolate. — A geographically restricted breeding group, such as is found in an isolated village community, within which random mating occurs. A **Social Isolate** is a breeding group restricted by class or caste.

Isolating Mechanisms. — Cytological, genetic, anatomical, physiological, or ecological causes which prevent or reduce sexual activity as between two or more groups of organisms.

Isolation. — The separation of one group from another within a species so that mating between the groups is prevented. **Geographic** — is separation due to geographical features, *e g.* existence of separate races on separate islands. Geographic isolation is divisible into **spatial** — and **topographical** —. **Habitat** —, or **Ecological** —, occurs as between groups which feed on different hosts, or between parasites on different hosts; territoriality is a form of habitat isolation **Seasonal** — is brought about by differences in flowering time or in mating periods **Genetic** — is due to such causes as translocations, inversions and similar sterility barriers

Isolation Distances. — For distances recommended in preventing seed contamination by spatial isolation, *see* Appendix 9.

Isomar. — A line showing the geographic distribution of races with equal phenotypic manifestation; phenocontour; isophene.

Isomere. — A homologous part.

Isomery. — Having an identical number of individual parts in each of several places (*e.g* in floral whorls).

Isometry. — Similar growth-rate, growth of a part at a standard rate or at the same rate as the whole.

Isomorphism. — Having a similar form and appearance. Adj. **Isomorphic, Isomorphous.**

Isophase. — Pleiotropy, *q v.*

Isophene. — Isomar, *q.v.*

Isophenous. — Belonging to the same phenotype.

Isoploid. — (i) Having an even number of sets of chromosomes in the somatic cells. (ii) An individual of this type; isopolyploid.

Isopolls. — Lines connecting points of equal pollen percentages during equivalent periods of time, applied only to fossil pollen (CAIN, 1944)

Isopolyploidy. — The state of having an even number of sets of chromosomes in the somatic cells, *e.g.* tetraploids, hexaploids, etc.

Isotropic. — Of an egg: having no predetermined axis.

Isozygotic. — Homozygous at a given locus and carrying the same alleles.

Isozygoty. — Genetical identity.

J_1, J_2, J_3. — First, second and third generations of inbreeding

Jarovization — Vernalization; the treatment of seeds, before sowing, by any technique designed to hasten the flowering period of the plants to which the seeds give rise

Jordanon. — A small species, or subspecies, having little variability.

Kakogenic. — Dysgenic; tending to impair the hereditary qualities of the race, or strain

Kapeller-Adler Test. — A pregnancy test based on estimation of histidine in the urine

Karenchyma. — The nuclear sap

Karyaster. — A group of chromosomes radially arranged and star-like in appearance.

Karyenchyma. — Nuclear sap; the more fluid contents of the nucleus.

Karyochylema. — The nuclear sap

Karyogamy. — Fusion of two nuclei.

Karyokinesis. — Mitosis, the process of nuclear division in which daughter nuclei are formed each having a chromosome complement similar to that of the original nucleus *See* under Mitosis.

Karyological Races. — Races of a species all having the same chromosome number which differs from that typical of the species.

Karyology. — The science of the structure and function of nuclei

Karyolymph. — The nuclear sap; karyenchyma

Karyolysis. — The apparent dissolution of the nucleus during mitosis

Karyomere. — A small vesicle in the nucleus (after nuclear division) which usually encloses a single chromosome.

Karyomerite. — Karyomere, *q.v.*

Karyomicrosome. — A microsome located in the nucleus.

Karyomites. — Chromosomes, chromophilic bodies, typically constant in number in any particular species, into which the nucleus resolves itself during cell division.

Karyomitome. — The nuclear reticulum.

Karyomitosis. — Nuclear division by mitosis.

Karyon. — A nucleus; the most constant constituent of animal and plant cells which reproduces by mitosis and contains the chromosomes.

Karyoplasm. — Nucleoplasm; the denser protoplasm of which nuclei are composed as distinct from the less dense cytoplasm outside the nuclear membrane.

Karyoplast. — A cell nucleus.

Karyorhexis. — Nuclear fragmentation.

Karyosome. — A vague term meaning a chromosome, a special form of nucleolus or even a nucleus.

Karyosphere. — Part of the nucleus into which the chromosomes have contracted (DARLINGTON).

Karyota. — Nucleate cells.

Karyotheca. — The nuclear membrane; the membrane surrounding the nucleus, dividing the nucleoplasm from the cytoplasm.

Karyotin. — Chromatin; a deeply staining substance in the nucleus; the part of the chromosome that stains deeply with basic dyes during cell division.

Karyotype. — (i) A group of individuals having the same chromosome number, homologous chromosomes throughout the group being characterized by an approximately similar series of gene loci arranged in the same linear order. (ii) The chromosome complement characteristic of such a group. *cf.* Genotype.

Katachromasis. — A general term for the changes which take place during telophase and the formation of daughter nuclei.

Katagenesis. — Devolution; retrogessive evolution.

Kataphase. — A collective term for all the stages of mitosis which follow anaphase.

Key Gene. — A main gene or oligogene; a gene whose effect is sufficiently large to give evident mendelian ratios when examined against an approximately pure genetic background.

Kindred. — A group of individuals each of whom is related in some way, either by blood relationship or by marriage, to every other member of the group and, in so far as is or can be known at any given time from the available records, to no other person (SOUTHWICK, 1939).

Kinetic Body. — A minute granular structure occurring in the immediate vicinity of the centromere.

Kinetic Constriction. — Centromere; spindle attachment; insertion region; kinetochore; a non-staining, localized region in each chromosome which remains single for some time after the rest of the chromosome has divided, and which, at metaphase, appears to be attached to the spindle 'fibre'.

Kinetochore. — Centromere *See* Kinetic Constriction

Kinetogenesis. — A theory of evolution based on the hypothesis that evolutionary changes take place in response to animal movements. *cf.* Lamarckism.

Kinetosomes. — Granular or rod-like bodies often aggregated to form plate-like bodies, which occupy the spindle-poles in the sporogenetic mitosis of mosses (ALLEN; WILSON).

Kinomere. — Kinetic constriction, *q v.*

Kinoplasm. — A modified type of cytoplasm which appears in the form of strands (*e.g.* spindle fibres) or of channels in the unmodified cytoplasm

Kinosome. — A minute body sometimes seen in the centromere in such cases there being one kinosome on each chromonema where it passes through the spindle attachment region.

Kleistogamous. — Cleistogamous; with close fertilization, this taking place within the unopened flowers.

Klon. — A group of individuals all derived asexually from a single organism, clone.

Knight-Darwin Law. — The hypothesis that "nature abhors perpetual self-fertilization" and that "nature intended that a sexual intercourse should take place between neighbouring plants of the same species."

Labile Genes. — Genes which are constantly mutating.

Lactoflavine. — Part of the vitamin B_2 complex.

Lagging. — Delay in moving from the equator to the poles at anaphase, of one or more chromosomes so that these become excluded from the daughter nuclei.

Lamarckism. — The theory that evolution is brought about by the inheritance of acquired characters.

"Lampbrush" Chromosomes. — A type of chromosome appearing during the prolonged pachytene stage which occurs in certain yolky eggs. Each chromosome comprises two greatly enlarged chromatids whose chromomeres give rise to looped filaments

Lanthanin. — A vague term designating one or more particular structural components of the nucleus; linin.

Lata-type. — A mutant individual possessing one or more supernumerary chromosomes in its nuclei.

Latent. — Used of characters whose genes exist in the germplasm of an individual without being phenotypically evident.

Lateral Gynandromorph. — An individual, half of whose body is male and the other half female.

Lateral Trabant. — *See* under Trabant.

Layering. — A method of vegetative propagation which consists in bending a branch over, so that part of it can be covered with earth to encourage adventitious rooting

Leptonema. — The long, fine, single, unpaired chromosome thread at the leptotene stage (beginning of prophase) of meiosis.

Leptotene. — An early stage of the prophase of meiosis when the chromosomes are in the form of single fine threads

Lethal Factors. — Genes which, in the homozygous state, have such a marked deleterious effect that such homozygous organisms are inviable. Where the homozygote is capable of survival but with impaired efficiency the factors responsible are termed **Semi-Lethal.**

"Limited" Chromosomes. — Chromosomes which occur only

in nuclei of the germ-line and never in somatic nuclei. (Such cases have been reported in *Sciara* by METZ)

Line Breeding — A special form of inbreeding to one ancestor, in which the mating of animals related in a lesser degree than that described as in-breeding is practiced. No hard and fast line can be drawn between line-breeding and in-breeding.

Line of Breeding. — A rather indefinite term used somewhat loosely, applied to a group of individuals which have descended from one individual; used more frequently and correctly with reference to male lines of descent (WINTERS).

Linin. — A vague term designating one or more particular structural components of the nucleus

Linkage. — Association of genetic factors, due to the genes being in the same chromosome. *See*, also, Sex Linkage, Complete Sex Linkage and Partial Sex Linkage

Linkage Map. — Chromosome map; a diagram of the relative position of the genes in a chromosome

Linkage Value. — Recombination Fraction, *q v.*

Liquor folliculi. — An albuminous, alkaline, yellowish fluid filling the space between the ovum and the epithelial cells of the Graafian follicle.

Localization. — The limiting of chiasma formation to a particular portion of the paired chromosome.

Lock and Key Theory. — The theory, propounded by DU-FOUR, that the female and the male genitalia of the same species (at least in insects) are so exactly fitted to each other that even slight deviations in the structure of either make copulation physically impossible (*cf* DOBZHANSKY, 1941).

Locus. — The fixed position of a gene in its chromosome.

Long-day Plants. — Plants whose flowering-time is hastened by an increased period of daylight (normally more than twelve hours). Opp Short-day Plants.

Loss, Arber's Law of. — *See* under Arber.

Luploidion. — A species whose individuals are sexually reproductive and which is composed of segments with a common origin arranged in a euploid series; the segments are morphologically separable although similar in appearance but, because of differential responses in various environmentals, appear to intergrade (CAMP & GILLY).

Luteal Hormone. — Progesterone; a sex hormone which has a specific action on the uterine endometrium.

Luteinisation. — The formation, in large amount, of corpora lutea in the ovary (MOTTRAM, 1944).

M I, M II. — The first and second metaphases respectively, in meiosis.

Macrandrous. — Having unusually large male organs.

Macroconjugant. — Macrogamete, *q.v.*

Macro-evolution. — (i) The evolutionary process as considered over long periods of time and large 'groups' of organisms. (ii) GOLDSCHMIDT's term for the large-scale evolution which is supposed to give rise to new species and genera by means of 'systemic mutations' which involve a radical change in the primary chromosomal pattern or reaction system. *cf.* Micro-evolution

Macrogamete. — The bigger of two conjugating gametes (typically the female).

Macro-mutation. — A 'mutation' bringing about a simultaneous change in a number of different characters.

Macront. — A mother-cell which gives rise to macrogametes.

Macronucleus. — The larger of the two nuclei in the *Infusoria,* the "vegetative" nucleus.

Macrosomes. — Alveolar spheres which occur in alveolar protoplasm

Macro-pyrenic. — (i) Having nuclei which are considerably larger than the average for the species, individual, etc. (ii) An individual of this type.

Macrospecies. — Large species typically having considerable variability but well differentiated from other related species.

Macrospore. — Megaspore, *q.v.*

Maiosis. — Meiosis, *q v.*

Male Haploidy. — A system of sex-determination in which the haploid individuals are males whilst the diploid condition determines femaleness.

Male-limited Chromosomes. — Chromosomes which occur only in nuclei of the male germ-line, never in somatic nuclei of either sex, and never in nuclei of the female germ-line; androsomes.

Male Parthenogenesis. — The development of an individual from a male gamete without fertilization having taken place.

Male Pronucleus. — The generative nucleus of a male gamete.

Mantle Fibres. — Spindle fibres; fibres which appear to connect the centromeres to the poles of the spindle during cell division. These are possibly artefacts of fixation which correspond positionally with some latent 'structure' of the spindle cytoplasm but which do not exist as definite fibres until coagulated by chemical reagents.

Mass Mutation. — A sudden marked spurt of mutability in a population.

Mass-pedigree Selection. — A form of mass selection in which individual plants are selected when conditions favour selection for a given character; selection in the following season may be of individual plants or of complete progenies, according to the seasonal conditions. In the following year the selections are all sown in bulk.

Mass Selection. — A form of breeding in which individuals, chosen for certain characteristics, are bulked together in the following generation.

Matched S Gene. — Any S gene ($q\,v$) which is represented in both the style and pollen in a given pollination (LEWIS)

Maternal Inheritance. — Inheritance from mother to offspring unaffected by inheritance from the father (J. Heredity).

Matriclinous. — Matroclinous, $q\,v.$

Matrix. — The peripheral more stainable portion of a chromosome.

Matroclinal Inheritance. — Inheritance in which the offspring resembles the female parent more closely than the male. Opp. Patroclinal

Matroclinic, Matroclinal. — Matroclinous, $q.v.$

Matroclinous. — Matriclinous; resembling the mother more closely than the father. Opp. Patroclinous, Patriclinous.

Matromorphic. — Similar in appearance to the female parent.

Maturation. — (i) The formation of gametes by meiosis. (ii) The period which elapses between pollination and the ripening of the fruit.

Maturation Division. — A form of nuclear division in which the chromosome complement of the nuclei is reduced from the diploid (2n) number to the haploid (n). *See* Meiosis

Mature-plant Resistance. — A term applied particularly to resistance to stem rust in the stages from heading to maturity where this resistance is not correlated with seedling reaction (HAYES & IMMER).

M-chromosome. — (i) A chromosome with a median or submedian centromere. (ii) A micro-chromosome.

Mean. — The sum of a group of observations divided by the number in the group.

Mean-square Error. — *See* Appendix 1

Mediastinum Testis. — The central core of a testis

Mediocentric. — Having a median or sub-median centromere.

Mega-evolution. — Macro-evolution, *q v.*

Megagamete. — Macrogamete; the larger of two conjugating gametes (typically the female).

Megaheterochromatic. — A species or individual which differs from its group in having more heterochromatin Opp. Microheterochromatic.

Meganucleus. — Macronucleus; the larger of two nuclei in a cell; the "vegetative" nucleus.

Megasporangia. — Ovules, *q.v.*

Megaspore. — The larger type of spore in heterosporous higher plants This, in the seed plants, gives rise to the embryo-sac.

Megasporocyte. — The diploid cell in the ovary from which the four haploid megaspores are formed — the embyro-sac mother-cell.

Meiocyte. — A cell whose nucleus has begun to divide by meiosis.

Meiomery — The state of having fewer than the normal number of parts Adj. **Meiomeric.** *cf.* Pleiomery.

Meiosis. — A form of mitosis in which the chromosome complement of the nuclei is reduced from the diploid (2n) number to the haploid (n). Typically, meiosis consists of the following stages —

1st Division.

(i) **Prophase.** (*a*) Leptotene: the chromosomes appear as long, fine, single, unpaired threads 2n in number (*b*) Zygotene: homologous chromosomes come together in pairs to form n bivalents (*c*) Pachytene each member of each paired zygotene chromosome splits longitudinally into two chromatids which remain closely associated (*d*) Diplotene. the four chromatids (= one bivalent) formed in pachytene, move apart in two pairs but these two pairs remain adherent in the region of chiasmata (*e*) Diakinesis: Pronounced shortening and thickening of the chromosomes now occurs.

(ii) **Metaphase.** The thickened chromosomes become arranged in the equatorial plane.

(iii) **Anaphase.** Repulsion between centromeres (spindle attachments) forces the chromosomes apart but the chromatids remain together, one pair from each bivalent going towards each pole

(iv) **Telophase.** — The chromosomes now take up water
and become surrounded by a nuclear membrane Telophase is
often followed by a short resting stage (interphase).
2nd **Division.**
This is a normal mitosis but with no prophase except when
an interphase follows telophase.

Meiotic Division. — Meiosis, *q v.*

Melanic. — Of darker colour.

Melanism. — Genetically controlled darkening of colour, *cf.*
Industrial Melanism

Mendel's Laws. — Mendel enunciated the following basic
principles of heredity· (*1*) That characters exhibit alternative
inheritance (dominant and recessive forms), (*2*) that each
reproductive cell receives but one member of a pair of determiners (genes) existing in the mature individuals; and
(*3*) that the reproductive cells combine at random (J. Heredity).

Mendelian Character. — A character the inheritance of which
follows MENDEL's Laws *i.e.* one showing allelomorphic inheritance.

Mendelism. — System of heredity based on MENDEL's Laws,
q.v.

Menopause. — The period during which the "change of life"
occurs in woman. During this period the ovaries atrophy and
the oestrus cycle is terminated.

Mental Ratio. — *See* under Intelligence Quotient.

Mericlinal Chimaera. — An incomplete periclinal chimaera;
a plant composed of two genetically different tissues one of
which partly surrounds the other.

Meristic Variations. — Differences in the number of parts,
segments or organs in the plant or animal body *e g.* variations
in the number of locules per boll in cotton.

Merocytes. — The nuclei derived from the supernumerary
sperm-nuclei which have failed to conjugate with the egg
nucleus in cases of physiological polyspermy (RUCKERT, WIL-
SON).

Merogamy. — A condition in which the gametes are smaller
than the vegetative cells, often of different structure, arising
by division from the gametocytes (WILSON).

Merogony. — The development and production of young from
a fertilized portion of an ovum containing no female pronucleus.
Where the male gamete is of a different species from the
female this process is called **Bastard Merogony.**

Merostathmokinesis. — Incomplete inhibition of the spindle (usually as a result of treatment with colchicine or some substance with similar effects). This may occur either through the failure of the cytoplasm to behave normally, or through the failure of the nucleus, this latter effect being termed **hemikinesis**.

Mesomitosis. — A form of nuclear division effected within the nuclear membrane, so that the cytoplasm takes no active part in the process

Metabolic Differentiation, Theory of. — The theory that sex determination is conditioned by the degree of metabolism of the developing individual

Metabolic Nucleus. — A 'resting' nucleus, *i e.* one which is not dividing.

Metabolic Stage. — The resting stage; the phase in the nuclear cycle when the nucleus is at rest in the sense of not dividing.

Metacentric Chromosome. — An isochromosome, *i e.* a chromosome composed of two exactly similar arms united by a centromere.

Metagenesis. — Alternation of generations; an alternation of a sexual with an asexual form, or, cytologically, the alternation of a haploid with a diploid stage.

Metakinesis. — Metaphase. *See* Mitosis.

Metaphase. — The stage of mitosis (or meiosis) during which the chromosomes lie in the equatorial plane of the spindle. *See* Meiosis and Mitosis

Metaphase Pairing Index. — The proportion of metaphase cells in which two particular chromosomes have paired, to the total number of cells examined (*cf.* Tobgy).

Metaplasia. — The production by the cells of one tissue, of a different tissue

Metaplasm. — A general term for non-living inclusions in the protoplasm

Metasyndesis. — Parasynapsis; the side-by-side conjugation of chromosomes at zygotene

Metaxenia. — The influence sometimes exerted by pollen on the maternal tissues of a fruit. *cf* Xenia.

Methyl Testosterone. — *See* under Androgens.

Metoestrus. — The period following oestrus.

Microcentrum — The central part of the astral system.

Microchromosomes. — Originally a pair of fragment chromosomes in the *Hemiptera* characterized by much delayed synapsis. Now often used of any abnormally small chromosomes. M-chromosomes

Microchromosomic Chromocentra. — The heterochromatin on either side of the centric constriction.

Microconjugant. — Microgamete, *q v*

Micro-evolution. — (i) The evolutionary process as considered over short periods of time and limited to small 'groups' of organisms. (ii) Used by GOLDSCHMIDT to denote evolution which is dependent on gene mutation and recombination, as opposed to macro-evolution, *q.v.*

Microgamete. — The smaller of two conjugants; the male gamete Opp Macrogamete.

Micro-grafting. — A method by which small embryos, either from artificial cultures or from mature seeds, may be grafted onto normal stocks with protection against evaporation (*cf.* BLAKESLEE).

Microheterochromatic. — An individual or species which differs from its group in having less heterochromatin.

Micro-mutation. — A mutation, or sudden heritable change, at a single gene locus.

Micron. — 0 001 mm.

Micronucleus. — The small reproductive nucleus of many *Protozoa* as distinct from the large vegetative nucleus or macronucleus.

Micropyle. — (1) The aperture through which the pollen-tube penetrates the ovule (11) The aperture in the membrane of the egg through which the sperm usually penetrates the ovum.

Micropyrenic. — (i) Having nuclei which are considerably smaller than the average for the species (or individual, etc.). (11) An individual of this type

Microspecies. — A small species or Jordanon.

Microsphere. — The centrosome, *q.v.*

Microsporangia. — Pollen-sacs.

Microspore. — The haploid cell from which a single pollen grain develops. *See* Microsporocyte.

Microsporocyte. — Pollen Mother-cell, the cell which undergoes two meiotic divisions to produce four microspores.

Micton. — A species of wide distribution, the results of hybridization between individuals of two or more species, all individuals are interfertile with themselves and with the ancestral genotype (CAMP & GILLY).

Mid-body. — The first stage in the formation of a cell-wall between daughter cells; the cell plate.

Middle Piece. — A vague term signifying the middle region of a sperm

Millimicron. — 0 000001 mm

Milt. — Testes of fishes.

Mimetism. — Mimicry, *q v.*

Mimic Genes. — Two or more non-allelomorphic genes which produce similar or identical effects.

Mimicry — Resemblance of one species to a second species due to natural selection. *See* Batesian —; Mullerian —.

Miscegenation. — Interbreeding as between different varieties.

Misogamy. — Reproductive isolation.

Mitochondria. — *See* Chondriosomes.

Mitogenetic Radiation. — Radiation supposed to emanate from certain growing tissues and to induce mitosis in other tissues.

Mitogenic Rays. — Mitogenetic Radiation, *q v.*

Mitome. — The protoplasmic reticulum as opposed to the ground substance.

Mitoschisis. — Mitosis, *q v.*

Mitosis. — The process of nuclear division in which daughter nuclei are formed each having a chromosome complement similar to that of the original nucleus. Mitosis is divisible into the following stages:

(i) **Prophase.** — Thin, double threads appear in the nucleus and these contract and thicken. Each double thread is a chromosome, split into two chromatids At this stage there are 2n chromosomes (4n chromatids) present.

(ii) **Prometaphase.** — Where a centrosome is present this now separates, the two halves moving to opposite sides of the nucleus, but remaining 'joined' by the spindle. The nuclear membrane disappears

(iii) **Metaphase.** — The chromosomes now arrange themselves in the equatorial plate

(iv) **Anaphase.** — Division of the centromeres now takes place and the two halves of each centromere repel each other, forcing the chromatids apart towards opposite poles of the spindle. (The chromatids are now called 'daughter chromosomes'). The equatorial region of the spindle now elongates (the 'stem body') thus moving the two sets of daughter chromosomes still further apart.

(v) **Telophase.** — The chromosomes elongate and take up water becoming less and less easily discernible. Each group becomes surrounded by a nuclear membrane and is now a daughter nucleus with 2n chromosomes.

Mitotic Division. — Mitosis, *q v.*

Mixis. — Fertilization as between specialized gametes with the concomitant phenomena of an alternation of a diploid and a haploid phase.

Mixochimaera. — An individual obtained by mixing the protoplasm of two individuals. (Such individuals have been formed artificially in certain fungi)

Mixochromosome. — A newly fused chromosome pair produced by syndesis (zygotene)

Mixoploid. — An individual in which polyploid and non-polyploid tissues are intermingled; also used adjectivally as "mixoploid tissue", "mixoploid branch".

Mixovariation. — A variation due to genetic segregation or to recombination.

Mock-dominance. — The apparent dominance of a recessive gene due to its being in the hemizygous state so that its dominant allele is absent, pseudo-dominance.

Modificational Plasticity. — *See* Plasticity, Modificational.

Modifier Complex. — An assemblage of genes which conjointly affects the degree of expression of a given pair of alleles. (HARLAND, 1941).

Modifying Factors or Modifiers. — Factors which modify the effect of a major factor but which have no effect in its absence

Molecular System of Heredity. — The cytoplasmic system of heredity in which units of heredity, or determinants, are carried by the cytoplasm. *cf.* Nuclear System and Corpuscular System.

Monad. — A single cell arising (instead of a tetrad) from a spore mother-cell as a result of the failure of meiosis.

Monadelphous. — Having all the stamen filaments joined in a single bundle.

Monandrous. — (1) Possessing only a single stamen. (ii) Having a single male mate.

Monandry. — State of being monandrous, *q.v.*

Monaster. — A single aster, formed in monocentric mitosis, which does not ordinarily give rise to an amphiaster (WILSON).

Monobasic. — Having similar genoms, *e.g.* diploids, autopolyploids.

Monocarpic. — Bearing fruit only once then dying.

Monocentric. — Having a single centromere.

Monocentric Mitosis. — Mitosis in which a uni-polar spindle (half-spindle) is formed.

Monochlamidius Chimaera. — Monochlamydeous chimaera, *q.v.*

Monochlamydeous. — Possessing a calyx but no corolla.

Monochlamydeous Chimaera. — A chimaera in which the epidermis forms one component and the inner tissues the other. *cf.* Dichlamidius.

Monochorionic. — With only one chorion as in monozygotic ('identical') twins.

Monoclinous. — Having perfect (hermaproditic) flowers.

Monodelphous. — Monadelphous, *q.v.*

Monoecious. — Hermaphrodite; with male and female elements on the same plant, but in different flowers.

Monoestrus. — Having only a single oestrus cycle per year or per breeding season.

Monofactorial. — Controlled by. a single factor or gene.

Monogametic. — Producing gametes of only one kind in regard to their properties of sex determination.

Monogamous. — Having only one mate. N. **Monogamy.**

Monogenesis. — (i) Reproduction by asexual means. (ii) Theory which supposes evolution to have taken place from a single entity.

Monogenetic. — Reproducing asexually.

Monogenic. — (i) Producing offspring of only one sex. (ii) Hemizygous. (iii) Controlled by a single gene; monofactorial. N. **Monogeny.**

Monogenist. — One who holds that all humans are derived from one common pair of ancestors. *cf.* Polygenist.

Monogenomic Species. — A species whose gametes carry a single set of chromosomes *i.e.* not a polyploid species.

Monogony. — Asexual reproduction (animals).

Monogynous. — Of a male animal, consorting with only one female; of a flower, having only one pistil. N. **Monogyny.**

Monohybrid. — A cross between parents differing in respect of a single gene, or a single specified gene.

Monohybrid Heterosis. — Hybrid vigour due to heterozygosity at a single gene locus.

Monokaryon. — Any nucleus which has only a single centriole.

Monomeric. — Carrying a dominant gene at only one of two duplicate loci. *cf.* Dimeric.

Monomerical Inheritance. — Inheritance in which a character is governed by a single allelomorphic pair of genes, as opposed to inheritance due to polymeric genes, *q.v.*

Monophyletic. — (i) Descendants of a single interbreeding group of populations *i.e.* of a single species (MAYR). (ii) Having a single line of descent from one common parent form. *cf.* Polyphyletic.

Monoploid. — (i) Haploid. (ii) The basic haploid chromosome number in a polyploid series.

Monoploid Hybrid. — A hybrid carrying a single genom made up of chromosomes and portions of chromosomes from different sources. (Occurs in certain algae and bryophytes).

Monosome. — The unpaired sex chromosome

Monosomic. — A diploid in which one chromosome is missing from the complement.

Monospermy. — Fertilization by only one spermatozoon.

Monostigmatous. — Possessing only one stigma.

Monostylous. — With only one style.

Monothelious. — Of a female animal having more than one mate

Monotocous. — Giving birth to a single offspring after each gestation *cf*. Multiparous.

Monotypic. — Having only one form

Mon-oval Twins. — Uniovular, monozygotic, or identical twins, *i e* those arising from a single egg.

Monozygotic. — Of twins, triplets, etc. originating from one fertilized egg, which gives rise to two or more individuals.

Morbific Factor. — A genetic factor which governs the predisposition of an individual to any particular disease or which directly controls a particular morbid condition (*e.g.* haemophilia)

Morgan. — A unit measure of the comparative linear distance between genes, each morgan is equal to one percent of crossing-over.

Morphogenesis. — The developmental history of an organism or of a part of an organism The evolution of structures.

Morphoplasm. — Formative protoplasm A modified type of cytoplasm which appears in the form of strands (*e.g.* spindle fibres) or of channels in the unmodified cytoplasm

Mosaic. — A chimaera, particularly when produced by repeated mutation

Mother-cell. — A diploid cell whose nucleus divides meiotically to give four haploid nuclei. The sperm mother-cell is called the spermatocyte and the egg mother-cell the oocyte, in animals.

Mule. — The offspring of a male donkey and a mare.

Mullerian Mimicry — Resemblance as between two unpalatable species. In this form of mimicry the two species, by sharing a similar type of aposematic coloration, share jointly the risk of mistaken attack by a predator *cf* Batesian — .

Multigenic. — Controlled by a number of genes; multifactorial.

Multipara. — A woman who has given birth to two or more children.

Multiparous. — Bearing several individuals at a single birth.

Multiple Alleles. — A series of genes each differing from the other but all alternatively sited at the same chromosomal locus.

Multiple Allelomorphs. — Multiple alleles, *q.v.*

Multiple Cross. — A cross in which a hybrid is crossed with a type of different origin from either of its parents; often a cross between hybrids of different origin. *cf.* Double F_1.

Multiple Diploid. — Allopolyploid.

Multiple Factor Hypothesis. — A hypothesis which explains the blending inheritance often found in quantitative characters on the assumption that there is a series of independent cumulative genes governing such a quantitative trait.

Multiple Factors. — Two or more pairs of factors with a complementary or cumulative effect. By extension, any factors working together to produce a single result.

Multipolar Spindle. — A type of spindle with several poles found in cancerous tissue.

Multivalent. — A group of more than two chromosomes which are held together at meiosis by mutual attraction or by chiasmata (WHITE).

Murphy's Rule. — Island birds have longer bills than related mainland races (MAYR, 1942).

Mutant. — An individual which has suddenly acquired a heritable variation not present in the parent form and, by extension, the offspring of such an individual as 'mutant race', 'mutant strain'.

Mutation. — A sudden change in the hereditary make-up. *cf.* Inter-genic Changes, Intra-genic Changes.

Mutation Pressure. — The continued production of a gene by mutation (ALTENBURG, 1945).

Mutation Rate. — The frequency with which mutations take place in a given variety or species, or the frequency with which any specified mutation occurs in a given population.

Mutation Trend. — A series of slight gene mutations in the same direction resulting in gradual intensification of a character change (PINCHER, 1946).

Mutual Translocation. — Reciprocal transfer, or crossing-over, between the terminal portions of two non-homologous chromosomes.

Myrmecophilous. — Pollinated by means of ants.

n, 2n.— The gametic and somatic (zygotic) chromosome numbers respectively.

Naphthaleneacetic Acid. — A growth regulating substance which has been used with considerable effect, at low concentrations, in the induction of flowering (*cf* OVERBEEK, 1945).

Napierian Logarithms. — For conversion figures see Appendix 1.

Natural Logarithms. — Napierian logarithms, *q.v.*

Natural Selection. — The automatic selection which takes place under natural conditions by reason of the death or partial inhibition of individuals less fitted to thrive under the conditions obtaining.

Neanic. — Pertaining to primitive or larval growth

"Necktie" Association (of chromosomes). — Two attached bivalents connected by a 'hump' on each of them Such a hump is thought to be an indication that chiasmata cannot be terminalized, either by reason of lack of homology at the ends of the chromosomes or through the inhibiting effect of secondary constrictions.

Necrohormones. — Products of degenerating nuclei which are thought to stimulate mitosis.

Neighbourhood — A population in which the individuals are neighbours in the sense that their gametes may come together (SEWALL WRIGHT).

Neocarpy — The flowering and fruiting of plants while still immature.

Neo-Darwinism. — A theory of evolution which, whilst taking account of modern genetic facts, postulates that natural selection is the chief agency in bringing about evolutionary processes

Neoergosterol. — A steroid, of the Vitamin D group, which shows oestrogenic properties.

Neoteinia. — Neoteny, *q.v.*

Neoteny. — The retention of phylogenetic larval characters in adult life (*e g. Amphibia*) ; the retention of juvenile characters in the adult, paedogenesis Adj. **Neotenous.**

Net-knots. — Karyosomes.

Netrum. — *See* Initial Spindle.

Neurobiotaxis. — A change in the position of nerve centres in the brain during phylogenetic evolution due to a change in the nerve-fibres from which any given nerve-centre habitually receives its impulses.

Neutrophilic. — Staining readily with neutral stains.

New Place Effect. — The effect whereby seed from one locality produces different results when grown in a different locality

New Reunion (of chromosomes) — Rejoining between a broken end and any other broken end except the one to which it was originally attached (NEWCOMBE).

Niacin. — A component of the vitamin B_2 complex.

Nicking. — A fortunate combination of genes which produces a more positive effect than the sum total of the single gene effects (PINCHER, 1946).

Nicotinamide. — One of the components of the vitamin B_2 complex.

Nicotinic Acid. — C_5H_4N COOH, one of the components of the vitamin B_2 complex.

Nidation. — The embedding of a fertilized ovum in the uterine wall.

Nomogenesis. — The theory that the evolution of organisms is the result of certain processes inherent in them and that it follows definite laws.

Non-adaptive Radiation. — The evolution of several closely related and morphologically divergent forms without apparent ecological diversification (CAIN, 1944).

Non-conjunction. — Failure of metaphase pairing

Non-disjunction. — The failure of a paired chromosome to separate at meiosis so that both members of the pair are carried to the same daughter nucleus.

Non-homologous Pairing. — Association of non-homologous parts of chromosomes at pachytene; *cf.* Torsion Pairing (McCLINTOCK, DARLINGTON).

Non-recurrent Parent. — Donor parent; that parent from which, by backcrossing, one or more genes are transferred to the backcross parent (recurrent parent). That parent of a hybrid which is not again utilized as a parent in backcrossing

Northocline. — A hybrid cline; an extension of the term cline (*q v.*) to cover the gradation of forms which occur in nature following inter-specific hybridization

Nucellar Embryony. — The purely vegetative development of cells in the nucellus or integument into the embryo sporophyte (DARLINGTON). The supernumerary embryos in Citrus are formed in this way. *See* under Reproduction.

Nuclear Budding. — The division of a nucleus into daughter nuclei by constriction.

Nuclear Disc. — The star-like group of chromosomes on the equatorial plate at metaphase.

Nuclear Division. — *See* under Mitosis, Meiosis and Amitosis.

Nuclear Membrane. — The membrane surrounding the nucleus, dividing the nucleoplasm from the cytoplasm.

Nuclear Plate. — The equatorial plate

Nuclear Sap. — The more fluid ground substance of the nucleus.

Nuclear Spindle. — *See* under Spindle Elements and Spindle Fibres.

Nuclear System of Heredity. — The normal, mendelian, system in which inheritance is controlled by genes located on the chromosomes, as opposed to the corpuscular (= plastid) system (*q v*) and the cytoplasmic (= molecular) system, *q.v.*

Nucleocentrosome. — An intra-nuclear division centre simulating a nucleolus, especially in *Protista* (WILSON).

Nucleochylema. — Nuclear sap, *q.v.*

Nucleohyaloplasm. — Nuclear sap, *q v*.

Nucleolar Organiser. — A specific chromomere responsible for developing the nucleolus (McCLINTOCK, DARLINGTON).

Nucleolinus. — A deeply staining granule within the nucleolus.

Nucleolus. — A darkly staining body occurring in the nuclei of most cells.

Nucleome. — The nuclear material of a single cell.

Nucleomicrosomes. — Nuclear chromatin granules.

Nucleoplasm. — The denser protoplasm of which nuclei are composed as distinct from the less dense cytoplasm outside the nuclear membrane.

Nucleoplasmic Ratio. — The volumetric ratio of nucleus to cytoplasm.

Nucleoprotein. — A special protein in cell nuclei thought by some to be the principal constituent of chromosomes (others hold chromosomin to be the principal constituent).

Nucleus. — The most constant constituent of animal and plant cells which reproduces by mitosis and contains the chromosomes.

Nulliplex. — Recessive, used of the bottom recessive for a given character in a polyploid (aaaa).

Nullisomic. — An organism having the genetic formula 2n—2, *i e* a diploid individual lacking one chromosome-pair.

Numerical Hybrid. — A hybrid produced by crossing two plants with different chromosome numbers.

Nyctanthous — Of flowers, opening at night.

Nyctigamous. — Of flowers those which open at night and close by day

O. — Used to denote the absence of a sex chromosome *e g.* XX and XO as compared with the XX and XY system of sex inheritance.

Octonary Hybrid. — A hybrid obtained by crossing two different quaternary hybrids such that all eight of its great-grand-parents are different.

Octoploid. — Having eight haploid sets of chromosomes in the somatic cells

Oestradiol. — An ovarian hormone which controls oestrus.

Ooestradiol dipropionate, — benzoate, — ethinyl. — *See* under Oestrogens

Oestrin. — Sometimes used in the sense of any oestrogen but usually restricted to natural oestrogens belonging to the steroid group (*cf.* ROBSON)

Oestrin-withdrawal Theory of Menstruation. — The theory that the fall in the oestrin level is the essential factor in the genesis of all types of menstrual bleeding (ROBSON).

Oestriol, — glucuronide. — *See* under Oestrogens

Oestrogenic Substances. — Oestrogens, *q.v.*

Oestrogens. — A group of hormonic substances, some natural and some synthetic, which are able to bring about oestrus The following are included in this group Oestradiol, — benzoate, — dipropionate, — ethinyl, Oestrone, Oestriol, — glucuronide, Stilboestrol, — dipropionate, Hexoestrol, Triphenyl-chloro-ethylene

Oestrone. — *See* under Oestrogens.

Oestroscope. — An instrument for measuring the viscosity of the cervical mucus which closes the os uteri. The oestroscope detects the onset of oestrus since the viscosity of the cervical mucus reaches its minimum at oestrus.

Oestrus. — The period of sexual desire in animals; rut

Offset. — A side shoot used as a means of vegetative propagation

Oleosome. — Any fatty inclusion in the cytoplasm.

Oligandrous. — With few stamens; oligostemonous.

Oligocarpous. — With few carpels.

Oligogenes. — Major genes controlling qualitative characters which show normal mendelian inheritance.

Oligopyrene. — Of spermatozoa having less than the normal complement of chromosomes.

Oligospermous. — Producing few seeds.

Oligostemonous. — With few stamens; oligandrous.

Oligotokous. — Producing few young.

Ontogeny, Ontogenesis. — The developmental history of an individual from fertilized egg to adult organism. Adj. **Ontogenetic.**

Ooblastema. — A fertilized ovum

Oocentre. — The division centre of an ovum.

Oocyte. — The egg mother-cell from which are produced, by the first meiotic division, the secondary oocyte and the polar body. The secondary oocyte is functional, the polar body generally divides once and the daughter polar bodies disintegrate

Oogamy. — The fusion, in fertilization, of gametes of unequal size, typically a large female gamete and a small active male gamete Adj **Oogamous.**

Oogenesis. — The origin and development of female gametes by maturation divisions from an ovary.

Oogonium. — (i) The female sexual apparatus of the algae and fungi. (ii) A cell from which primary oocytes are produced by mitosis.

Ookinesis. — The mitotic phenomena in the egg-cell during maturation and fertilization (WHITMAN; WILSON).

Ooplasm. — The cytoplasm of the oocyte or ovum.

Oosperm. — A fertilized egg; ooblastema.

Oosphere. — A female gamete prior to fertilization.

Oospore. — A fertilized ovum; oosperm; ooblastema.

Ootid. — The haploid egg cell after meiosis *cf* Spermatid.

Organic Selection, Theory of. — The hypothesis that an organism may become genetically adapted to particular conditions by first undergoing non-heritable modification so that any subsequent mutations which are favourable to the new conditions of life tend to be selected and fixed

Organogenesis, Organogeny. — The differentiation and development of organs.

Organophyly. — The developmental origin of organs.

Orientation. — The movement of chromosomes so that their centromeres lie axially with respect to the spindle, either as to their potential halves at mitosis (**auto-orientation**) or as

to members of a pair in meiosis (co-orientation) (DARLING-
TON).

Ornithophilous. — Pollinated by means of birds

Orthogamy. — The normal relations of male and female (CAR-
PENTER).

Orthogenesis. — Purposive, 'predetermined' evolution towards
a definite objective. A tendency to vary continuously in the
same direction

Orthoploid. — A polyploid with a balanced number of complete
chromosome sets   *cf* Aneuploid.

Orthoselection. — Selection which increases the likelihood of
the continuance of any particular adaptive trend. Selection
acting over a long period of time with a general trend in one
particular direction.

Orthospiral — A spiralization of such a type that no secondary
compensational twisting occurs in the fabric of the thread.
cf Anorthospiral

Outcross. — A cross (generally resulting from natural pollination) to an individual of a different strain, variety or type

Ovariectomy. — The surgical removal of an ovary or ovaries

Ovary. — The part of the flower which contains the ovules; the
immature fruit. In animals, a female gonad or reproductive
gland

Overstepping. — This occurs when an animal, during its own
ontogeny, passes through the ontogenetic stages of its ancestor
but beyond the final adult stage of that ancestor; hypermorphosis   *cf* Anaboly

Ovogenesis. — Oogenesis, *q v.*

Ovotestis. — A gonad which is composed, in part, of testicular
substance and, in part, of ovarian tissue.

Ovule. — A body containing a female gamete and which, after
fertilization, develops into a seed.

Ovum. — The female gamete or egg. Pl. **Ova.**

Oxychromatin. — (1) Linin, *q.v.* (ii) That part of the nucleus
which stains readily with acid dyes.

Oxyphilic. — Staining readily with acidic dyes.

P₁. — The first parental generation, $i.e.$ the parents of an F_1; P_2 the grand-parents.

Pachynema — The chromosome thread at pachytene.

Pachytene. — The third stage in the prophase of meiosis ($q.v.$) during which the paired zygotene chromosomes each split longitudinally into chromatids so that each bivalent of two chromosomes is composed of four chromatids.

Paedogamy. — Fertilization by gametes derived from the same parent cell following many nuclear divisions.

Paedogenesis — Reproduction, either sexual or asexual, by larval animals or by individuals which are not adult; neoteny.

Paedomorphosis. — The process whereby a new form of adult organization is produced which is endowed with high potential for further evolution. A form of evolution in which some of the more important steps have resulted from novelties which first manifested themselves in early stages of development of the ancestors ($cf.$ DE BEER).

Pairing of Chromosomes — (Active) the coming together of chromosomes at zygotene or (passive) the continuance of their association at the first metaphase of meiosis (DARLINGTON). **Somatic** ——— The lying of homologous chromosomes especially close to one another at metaphase of mitosis (DARLINGTON) **Secondary** ———. The side-by-side association of bivalent chromosomes at meiosis **Zygotene Pairing.** — See under Meiosis, Heterogenetic Pairing, Homogenetic ——, Homosynapsis.

Pairing Segment. — (Of a sex chromosome) The portion of a sex chromosome which is duplicated in the dissimilar chromosome-partner See under Partial Sex Linkage

Palaeogenetic. — Pertaining to the persistence of larval or embryonic characters into adult life; neotenous

Palaeogenetics. — The genetic interpretation of phenomena observed in fossils.

Palingenetic Stages. — The stages which, during the development of an animal from the egg, recapitulate the history of the race.

Palingeny. — Repetition of ancestral forms during embryony.

p-amino benzoic acid. — A component of the vitamin B_2 complex

Pangamy. — Indiscriminate or random mating. Adj. **Pangamic.**

Pangenesis, Theory of. — DARWIN's theory that gemmules, collected from the organs into the germ cells, are dispersed again to corresponding organs for whose nature they are responsible (SHULL)

Pangens. — DARWIN's hypothetical particles controlling inheritance *See* Pangenesis, Theory of.

Panmictic Unit. — A local population in which there is completely random mating.

Panmixia. — (i) Random inbreeding with no selectivity and unaffected by natural selection. (ii) The cessation of the effect of natural selection.

Panmixie. — Panmixia, *q v.*

Pantothenic Acid. — A component of the vitamin B_2 complex.

Parabiotic Twins. — Animals (typically *Amphibia*) which have been grafted together, in the embryonic stage, so that the subsequent development of each is potentially able to be affected by the hormones developed by the other.

Paracentric Inversion. — An inversion which, being located entirely within one chromosome limb, does not involve the centromere.

Paracme. — The phase in the developmental history of a race or of an individual when vigour is waning.

Paradesm, Paradesmose, Paradesmus. — An extra-nuclear filament connecting the division centres in the mitosis of flagellates (KAFOID & SWEZY; WILSON).

Parageneon. — A species with relatively little morphological or genetical variation throughout its range but which contains some aberrant genotypes; all its individuals are interfertile (CAMP & GILLY).

Paragenesis. — Fertility as between a hybrid and one or both of its parents the hybrid being otherwise sterile.

Paralinin. — The ground-substance of a nucleus.

Parallel Mutations. — Closely similar mutations occurring in two or more species of the same genus, and affecting homologous genes and homologous processes. Sometimes mutations involving homologous processes but non-homologous genes are included under parallel mutations.

Paranuclein. — The substance of which nucleoli are composed.

Paraplasm. — Passive cell material.

Parastamen, Parastemon. — A sterile stamen.

Parasynapsis. — The side-by-side conjugation of chromosomes at the zygotene stage of meiosis.

Parasyndesis. — Parasynapsis, *q.v.*

Paravariation. — A modification or acquired variation developed during the life of the individual as a result of environmental causes and not heritable.

Paripotency. — Similarity of basic evolutionary potentiality between different species.

Parthenapogamy. — The conjugation or fusion of two somatic nuclei.

Parthenocarpy. — The formation of fruit without fertilization and without seeds, or with embryo-less seeds.

Parthenogamy. — Fusion of two female gametes.

Parthenogenesis. — (*See* also under Reproduction). The development of an organism from a female or a male gamete without fertilization. There are two types:

(i) **Diploid Parthenogenesis**, in which the reduction division of meiosis is abortive so that diploid ova are formed which, later, may develop without fertilization.

(ii) **Haploid Parthenogenesis**, in which normal ova with the gametic chromosome number develop without fertilization. Individuals produced by haploid parthenogenesis may have n or 2n chromosomes in their body-cells according to whether the unfertilized ovum does or does not double its chromosome number as the first step in development.

Parthenosperm. — A sperm capable of developing as a zygote without having fused with a female gamete.

Parthenote. — A haploid individual arising parthenogenetically.

Partial Dominance. — A reduced dominance characterized by the production of an intermediate phenotype in individuals heterozygous for the gene concerned; semi-dominance.

Partial Sex Linkage. — This occurs when the gene concerned is located on the homologous region of the X- or Y-chromosome so that crossing-over between the X- and Y-chromosomes can transfer the gene from one to the other.

Particulate Inheritance. — That in which distinctive characters from both parents appear in their offspring; mendelian inheritance.

Parturition. — The process of giving birth in viviparous animals.

Passive Adaptation. — Pre-adaptation, *q.v.*

Pathotype. — A group of individuals all exhibiting the same pathological condition.

Patriclinic, Patriclinous. — Patroclinous, *q v.* Opp Matroclinous.

Patroclinal Inheritance. — Inheritance in which the offspring resembles the father more closely than the mother.

Patroclinic. — Resembling the father more closely than the mother

Patroclinous. — Patroclinic, *q v.*

Patrogenesis — The production of a 'zygote' whose chromatin is derived solely from the male gamete

Patrogony. — Modificational adaptation during embryo or larval development

Patromorphic. — Similar in appearance to the male parent.

Pedigree. — A record or history of the ancestry of an individual, strain or variety.

Peloria, Pelory. — Reversion, on the part of an individual, to the production of regular flowers, when the species typically has asymmetrical flowers Adj. **Peloric.**

Penetrance. — The percentage frequency with which a gene produces any effect at all *See* Complete Penetrance, Penetrance, Reduced; Incomplete Penetrance *cf.* Expressivity.

Penetrance, Reduced — A reduction in the number of individuals in any one phenotype though the number in the corresponding genotype is not reduced, *i.e* the particular gene or genes involved, though present, are not always manifest.

Penis. — The intromissive copulatory organ of the male mammal.

Pentagynous. — Of a flower having five styles

Pentandrous. — Of a flower having five stamens.

Pentaploid. — Having five haploid sets of chromosomes in the somatic cells

Perfect. — Of a flower possessing both stamens and pistils, *i.e.* hermaphroditic.

Perforatorium. — A specialised pointed portion of the achrosome, *q v.*

Perianth. — The calyx and corolla collectively.

Pericarp. — The wall of a fruit, when derived from the ovary wall, consisting of three layers: exocarp, mesocarp and endocarp.

Pericentric Inversion. — An inversion which involves the centromere.

Periclinal Chimaera. — A plant made up of two genetically different tissues, one being external to, and surrounding the other.

Perigynous. — Calyx, corolla and stamens borne on a rim of the receptacle so that they are on the same level as the ovary.

Periplast. — Cytoplasm, *q.v.*

Perisphere. — The peripheral portion of the attraction sphere.

Permanent Hybrid. — A hybrid which is pure breeding by reason of the suppression of certain phenotypes by lethal factors.

Perultimate Chromomere. — Telomere, *q.v.*

Petaliform. — Petal-like.

Petalody. — The state of having one or more of the floral whorls petaliform, in addition to, or instead of, the corolla.

Petaloid. — Petal-like.

Pfluger's Egg Cords. — Columns of cells which, in the embryo, grow from the germinal epithelium down into the stroma and which give rise, in the male, to the testes, and in the female to the ovaries.

pH. — A measure of hydrogen-ion concentration. pH less than 7 shows acidity, pH 7 is neutral and pH more than 7 alkaline.

Phaenogenetics. — Phenogenetics, *q.v.*

Phenocontour. — A line showing the geographic distribution of races with equal phenotypic manifestation; isomar.

Phenocontour Map. — A map showing the geographic distribution of the polymorphic forms of a species, areas with a similiar percentage of one form (as compared with the population) being marked off by phenocontours or isomars (isophenes).

Phenocopies. — Environmentally produced imitations of gene mutants.

Phenogenetics. — The study of ontogeny to find the stage of development at which the difference between types first becomes manifest (DE BEER). Developmental genetics; that part of genetics which deals with the genetic control of the development of the outward, visible or concrete characters of an organism. Adj. **Phenogenetic.**

Phenogens. — Units of a phenon which are intersterile but which can not be distinguished except by genetic analysis.

Phenological Isolation. — Biologic isolation of one species or group from the other members of the genus by reason of differences in time of flowering.

Phenon. — A species which is phenotypically homogeneous and whose individuals are sexually reproductive, but which is composed of intersterile segments (CAMP & GILLY).

Phenotype. — A group of individuals of similar appearance but not necessarily of similar genetic constitution

Phenotypic. — Appertaining to the physical make-up of an organism or group of organisms as distinct from their genetic make-up. The phenotypic effect of any particular gene on an organism is its outward, measurable, quantitative or qualitative effect on that organism.

Phenotypic Intersex — An organism which though of one sex in genetic origin, develops as a result of physiological changes, organs or tissues characteristic of the other sex.

Phenotypic Sex Determination. — A form of sex determination in which the influence of the environment in which the new individual develops over-rides any genetical sex-mechanism.

Photoperiodism. — The governing of season of flowering by the number of hours of daylight per day. *See* Long-day and Short-day plants. Adj. **Photoperiodic.**

Phyloephebic. — Pertaining to the phase of the life of a race or individual when vigour is at its peak.

Phylogenesis, Phylogeny. — The evolutionary history of a species, genus or race. Adj. **Phylogenetic.**

Phylogenetic Series. — An evolutionary chain of organisms, most of the members of which are usually extinct, which indicates the descent of present-day types from earlier forms.

Phylogeny. — Phylogenesis, *q.v.*

Phylogerontic. — Pertaining to the phase in the life of a race (or individual) when senescence has begun.

Phyloneanic. — Phyloephebic, *q v.*

Phylonepionic. — Pertaining to the phase in the life of a race when the race is still young and has not reached its peak of vigour.

Phytogenesis. — The evolution and development of plants.

Phytogenetics. — Plant genetics.

Phytoplasm. — Plant protoplasm.

Pin-eyed. — Having the stigma level with the throat of the corolla and the anthers below, enclosed within the corolla-tube.

Pistil. — The ovary style and stigma, collectively.

Pistillate Flower. — A female flower lacking stamens.

Placenta. — The membrane, or surface, bearing ovules in plants and in animals a structure formed by the union of the allantois and chorion with the uterine wall and providing for the respiration and nutrition of the foetus.

Planogamic. — With motile gametes.

Planosome. — A supernumerary chromosome resulting from non-disjunction of a bivalent in meiosis.

Plasma Membrane. — A film which surrounds the cytoplasm.

Plasmagel. — The more viscous portion of cytoplasm in contradistinction to the plasmasol, *q.v.*

Plasmagenes. — Determinants, or units of heredity, located in the cytoplasm. *cf.* Plasmon.

Plasmasol. — The more fluid portion of the cytoplasm in contradistinction to the plasmagel, *q.v.* This commonly lies within the denser plasmagel.

Plasmodesms. — Fine protoplasmic strands connecting neighbouring cells.

Plasmogamy. — Cytoplasmic fusion.

Plasmogony. — Abiogenesis, *q.v.*

Plasmon. — The system of hereditary units thought by some to exist in the cytoplasm, as opposed to the system of genes in the chromosomes. *cf.* Plasmagenes.

Plasmosome. — A darkly staining body occurring in the nuclei of most cells; nucleolus.

Plasome. — Biophore, *q.v.*

Plasticity. — The potentiality for further evolution.

Plasticity, Modificational. — The capacity of an organism, species, or group of organisms, to adapt itself to changes in the environment. *See* Stenoplastic and Euryplastic.

Plastid. — Any minute dense protoplasmic cell-inclusion.

Plastid System of Heredity. — The "corpuscular" system of heredity in which units of heredity, or determinants, are carried in the plastids. *cf.* Nuclear System and Cytoplasmic System.

Plastidome. — A collective term for all the plastids in a single cell.

Plastochondria. — Mitochondria.

Plastocont. — A rod-like or thread-like chondriosome; chondriocont.

Plastogamy. — Cytoplasmic fusion.

Plastogenes. — Determinants, or units of heredity, located in the plastids.

Plastomere. — The part of a spermatozoon in which the chondriosomes occur.

Plastosome. — A self-propagating body with low refraction occurring in the cytoplasm; chondriosome.

Pleiomery. — The state of having more than the normal number of parts. Adj. **Pleiomeric.** *cf.* Meiomery.

Pleiotropism. — The controlling of more than one character by a single gene. Adj. **Pleiotropic.** *See* under Genuine Pleiotropism.

Pleiotropy. — Pleiotropism, *q.v.*

Pleurotribe. — Of flowers· having the stamens and stigmas so arranged as to encourage cross-pollination by automatically rubbing against any insect visitor

Ploidy. — Duplication of the chromosome set.

Plurivalent — An association of more than two chromosomes held together by chiasmata.

P-M-C. — Pollen mother-cell, *q v*

Point Mutation. — A heritable change taking place at a single gene locus, presumably caused by chemical alteration of the individual gene; a mutation proper, transgenation or genovariation.

Polar Bodies. — Small cells produced during the two divisions of the oocyte nucleus in animals. *See* under Oocyte.

Polar Cap. — The radiating fibrillae or striae which appear at the nuclear poles at the commencement of nuclear division.

Polar Fusion Nucleus. — The product of the fusion of the two polar nuclei. This, after fusing with a male nucleus, gives rise to the endosperm

Polarization, Polarized Chromosomes. — *See* under Pole-field

Pole — The point at either end of the spindle, from which the spindle fibres radiate to the equator

Pole-field. — That side of a nucleus towards which the attachment constrictions of the chromosomes are orientated at late telophase and early prophase This orientation of the chromosomes with centromeres towards one side of the nucleus is termed 'polarization' and the chromosomes are said to be 'polarized.'

Pole-plates. — Condensed plate-like bodies at the ends of the spindle in certain forms of mitosis (HERTWIG, WILSON).

Pollen-grain. — A microspore which germinates to form the male gametophyte (pollen grain plus pollen-tube) which contains three nuclei, one of these fertilises the ovum, a second fuses with the two polar nuclei to form the endosperm, whilst the third (the tube-nucleus) degenerates

Pollen-lethals. — Genes which act directly on the pollen, preventing those pollen grains which carry them from functioning.

Pollen Mother-cells — Sporogenous cells which lie within the pollen-sac. They are derived from the hypodermal cells of the pollen-sac and each gives rise to a pollen tetrad, the individual cells of which develop without further division into pollen grains.

Pollen-tube. — The protoplasmic tube which grows out from a germinating pollen-grain and penetrates the stigmatic tissues passing down the style to fertilize an ovule.

Pollinate. — To place pollen on a stigma.

Pollination. — The act of placing pollen on the receptive surface of a stigma.

Polocyte, or first polar body. — The small degenerate sister cell of the secondary oocyte. This first polar body generally divides into two polar bodies which disintegrate.

Polyadelphous. — With stamens separate, or in more than two groups.

Polyallel Crossing. — Crossing each inbred line with every other inbred line, or with certain other inbred lines; an extension of diallel crossing to cover the simultaneous comparison of more than two sires.

Polyandrous. — (i) With twenty or more stamens per flower. (ii) having more than one male mate.

Polyarch. — A type of anastral spindle in higher plants that is multipolar from the beginning (STRASBURGER; WILSON).

Polycaryon, Polykaryon. — A polykaryotic individual.

Polycaryoptic. — Having multiple seed formation.

Polycaryotic, Polykaryotic. — Having several nuclei in the one cell.

Polychlamydeous Chimaera. — A periclinal chimaera in which the peripheral constituent is more than two thicknesses of cells.

Polychronism. — The independent origin of a species at more than one time (CAIN, 1944).

Polyclinal Chimaera. — A chimaera in which more than two components are involved.

Polyembryony. — The presence of more than one embryo in a seed: often one embryo is sexually produced and the remainder vegetatively by diploid parthenogenesis (*q.v.* under Parthenogenesis).

Polygamous. — (i) With both perfect and imperfect flowers present on the same plant. (ii) Of an animal: having more than one mate during one breeding season. N. **Polygamy.**

Polygenes. — (i) Linked combinations of the genes determining quantitative variation (MATHER). (ii) Minor genes controlling quantitative characters which individually have too small an effect to show clear segregation.

Polygenesis. — The production of a new type at more than one place or more than one time.

Polygenic Balance. — The harmonious balance, between the systems of polygenes in a species and the natural environment of that species built up as a result of natural selection and enabling the organisms to develop normally and competitively.

Polygenic Character. — A character whose inheritance is controlled by many genes each having an effect which is small compared with non-heritable variation (MATHER).

Polygenist. — One who believes in the multiple genesis of man *cf.* Monogenist.

Polygenom Hybrid. — A hybrid whose somatic nuclei carry more than two complete genoms comprising the genoms of two or more distinct species

Polygoneutic. — Producing several broods per season

Polygynous. — (i) Having numerous styles. (ii) Having more than one female mate at a time N. **Polygyny.**

Polyhaploid. — An organism formed by a halving of the chromosome number of a polyploid.

Polyhybrid. — An individual heterozygous for several genes. A hybrid produced by crossing two individuals differing in several genes.

Polykaryotic. — Polycaryotic, *q.v.*

Polymeric Genes. — Non-allelomorphic genes governing the same character and having a similar effect on it.

Polymorphism. — The occurrence together in the same habitat of two or more forms of a species in such proportions that the rarest of them cannot be maintained by recurrent mutation (FORD). If the proportion of one of these forms is increasing in the population, the phenomenon is called **Transient Polymorphism**, whereas a form which is maintained in a constant proportion by a balance of selective agencies exemplifies **Balanced Polymorphism.**

Polymorphism, Neutral. — Polymorphism which is dependent on the action of alleles which are approximately neutral as regards their survival value.

Polymorphism, Regional. — The existence of two or more distinct forms of a species which are located in different regions; geographic polymorphism.

Polynucleate. — Having several nuclei

Polyoestrus. — Having a recurrent cycle of oestrus periods in the one sexual season.

Polypetalous. — Having several distinct (separate) petals.

Polyphasy. — The existence of any sharply marked variations of a species occurring within the same habitat (FORD).

Polyphyletic. — The condition of a taxonomic group, usually a genus or higher category, the members of which have not come from the same phylogenetic stock. Polyphyletic groups represent mistaken classification, according to most concepts, because of convergent or parallel evolution (CAIN, 1944).

Polyphylogeny. — Lineage through several lines of descent.

Polyphyly. — The state of being derived or descended from several parent forms.

Polyploid. — An organism whose somatic nuclei contain more than two haploid chromosome sets. *See* Secondary Polyploid.

Polyploid Complex. — A group of forms which contains self-propagating secondary hybrids which have arisen from crosses between auto- and allopolyploid forms.

Polyploiding Agent. — A substance or treatment which, under given circumstances, is capable of inducing polyploidy. The following substances have been used successfully: Acenaphthene and various derivatives thereof; Apiol; Aurantia; Colchicine; Diphenylamine, Esters of naphthoic acid; Ethyl mercuric chloride in conjunction with 1:2·5:6-dibenzanthracene; Naphthaleneacetic acid; Paradichlorbenzene; Sanguinarine; Sulphanilamide; Veratrine sulphate.

Polyploidogenic Activity. — The capacity of a substance (or ray, etc.) to induce polyploidy.

Polyploidy, Partial. — The reduplication of small segments of chromosome so that the organism is polyploid as regards the reduplicated segments though normal as regards the remainder of the chromosome complement.

Polysepalous. — Having several distinct (separate) sepals.

Polysomaty — The production of somatic nuclei with multiples of the normal somatic chromosome number

Polysomy. — (i) A condition in which some, but not all, of the chromosomes in the set are present in the polyploid state. (ii) Aneuploidy. N. Polysomic.

Polysperm, Polyspermal, Polyspermous. — Many seeded, having numerous seeds in the one pericarp

Polyspermy. — (i) The entry into the ovum of more than one sperm. (ii) Multi-seeded state.

Polysporous. — Having many spores, or seeds.

Polystemonous. — Polyandrous; having numerous stamens.

Polytene Chromosomes. — Salivary gland chromosomes (*q v.*) in *Diptera.*

Polytocous. — Giving birth to several young at a time.

Polytypic. — Having several forms, or more than one form.

Position-effect. — In certain organisms it has been shown that the visible effect of a gene is to some extent dependent on its interactions with its near neighbours in the chromosome and that changes in position due to translocations, inversions, etc. can alter the nature of the outward expression of the gene.

Postheterokinesis. — A form of meiotic division characterized by failure of the sex chromosome to divide so that it passes to only one pole in the second spermatocyte division. *cf.* Preheterokinesis.

Post-reduction. — A halving of the chromosome number occurring in the second meiotic division as opposed to normal reduction ('pre-reduction') which occurs during the first meiotic division.

Potence. — The effect of the integrated dominance and interaction relations of all the polygenic allelomorphs within the possible combinations (WIGAN).

Potency (of a gene). — The capacity of a gene for manifesting its presence. *cf* Expressivity and Penetrance. **Partial potency** is synonomous with incomplete dominance.

Pre-adaptation. — The existence of a character which renders an organism potentially able to make use of a changed environment or to extend its original environmental limits.

Pre-adaptation, Constitutional. — Adaptation in which a species is, by its existing peculiarities, already modified to suit certain modes of life or particular types of environment

Pre-adaptation, Mutational. — Adaptation in which a mutant form or natural variety is, *ab initio*, adapted to certain special environmental conditions in which it either originates, or into which it might be thrown by chance.

Precession. — The passing of the sex chromosomes to the poles in meiosis before the autosomes

Precocity. — The property of the nucleus beginning prophase before the chromosomes have divided; characteristic of meiosis. **Differential** ———. The property of some chromosomes or their parts condensing, dividing or pairing in advance of the rest of the complement during prophase (DARLINGTON).

Precocity Theory. — DARLINGTON's theory that the main difference between meiosis and mitosis depends on the fact that in meiosis the chromosomes condense precociously out of the resting nucleus and therefore they pair (ALTENBURG, 1945).

Predetermination. — Non-genetic variations in form and size of seed.

Preformation. — *See* under Epigenesis

Pregnancy. — Gestation, the period between conception (fertilization) and the birth of the offspring.

Prehensile Flowers. — Flowers whose insect visitors grasp the style and stamens so as to cover their venters with pollen and so effect pollination (CARPENTER)

Preheterokinesis. — A form of meiotic division characterized by the sex chromosome passing undivided to one pole in the first spermatocyte division. *cf* Postheterokinesis.

Premunition. — Disease tolerance resulting from latent infection occurring early in the life of the individual.

Prepotence. — (i) The capacity, in a sire, of being able to transmit his characteristics to his offspring The term can also be used of the dam but more commonly refers to the sire. (ii) The capacity of a particular type of pollen to fertilize the ovules of any specific plant despite simultaneous competition from the plant's own pollen

Pre-reduction. — *See* under Post-reduction.

Presence and Absence Theory. — The theory that dominance indicates the presence of the particular gene concerned and recessiveness its absence.

Pressure. — The force with which selection is working on an organism *e g* low or high predator —, competition —, selection —, disease —.

Primary Constriction. — Centromere, *q v*.

Primary Mutant. — A plant with one extra normal chromosome, *i.e.* a trisomic plant

Proanthesis. — The production of flowers before the normal flowering season.

Probability. — *See* Progeny in Appendix 1

Probable Error. — This is equal to the variance (Standard error) multiplied by 0 67449.

Prochromocentric Heterochromatin. — The heterochromatin on either side of the centric constriction

Pro-chromosomes. — Separate masses of basichromatin in the resting nuclei, or in the presynaptic stages, supposed to be forerunners of the definitive chromosomes or centres for their formation (OVERTON, WILSON). That part of the heterochromatin which is situated on either side of the centromeric constriction (LEVAN). *See* Heterochromatin.

Procryptic Coloration. — Coloration of a protective nature.

Progamic Sex Determination. — Sex determination which is dependent on the size or physiological state of the ova as opposed to normal sex determination which is largely governed by the heterosomes.

Progeny Size. — *See* Appendix 1.

Progestin. — A term used to include all the hormones of the corpus luteum governing pregnancy (MOTTRAM, 1944).

Prolan. — A sex hormone occurring in some mammals during pregnancy (*e g.* in urine of pregnant women).

Proloestrum. — The period of sexual preparation which precedes heat, or oestrum.

Prometaphase. — The period, in mitosis or meiosis, between the disappearance of the nuclear membrane and the moment when the spindle is fully formed.

Prometatropy. — Obigatory cross pollination. Adj. **Prometatropic.**

Promitosis. — A simplified form of mitosis, found in *Protista*, in which the whole process takes place within the nuclear membrane.

Pronucleus. — The nucleus of an egg, sperm or pollen-grain.

Pro-oestrum. — The period of sexual preparation which precedes heat, or oestrum.

Prophase. — The first stage in mitosis or meiosis. For details *see* Mitosis and Meiosis.

Proplastids. — Primordial plastids occurring in meristematic tissue.

Prostate. — A gland situated around the urethra near the neck of the bladder. The prostatic secretion is added to the semen at the time of ejaculation.

Protandrous. — With anthers ripening before the stigmas. N. **Protandry.**

Protanthesis. — The commencement of flowering in an inflorescence.

Proteranthy. — The state of bearing flowers before the foliage unfolds.

Protogene. — PEARSON's term for a dominant allele as opposed to allogene.

Protogenesis. — Reproduction by budding.

Protogynous, Proterogynous. — With stigmas ripening (becoming receptive) before the anthers. N. **Protogny, Protogyny, Proterogyny.**

Protoplasm. — Living cell substance including the nucleus and cytoplasm

Protoplast. — The portion of a cell which is truly living; the protoplasm of one cell.

Protosome. — THOMPSON's (1931) term for the physical gene base, which, according to AGOL (1931) and DUBININ (1932), is divisible into a number of adjacent "gene centres" arranged in linear order along the axis of the chromosome. *cf*. Episome, Chromogene, Cytogene, Genosome.

Protozygote. — PEARSON's term for an organism homozygous for a particular dominant gene. *See* Allozygote.

Provenance. — The source, or place of origin, of any particular lot of seed

Proximal. — That part (of a chromosome) which is nearer the centromere than any specified other part.

Pseudapogamy. — The replacement of amphimixis by the conjugation of two ova or of an ovum and a nucleus of somatic origin, or of two somatic nuclei.

Pseudaposematic. — Pertaining to mimicry in which the warning coloration of a noxious type is the pattern which is copied.

Pseudapospory. — The mitotic formation of a diploid spore.

Pseudoalleles. — Genes which appear to be allelic to each other by reason of their being closely linked. Such genes are said to show **Pseudoallelism.**

Pseudodominance. — Mock-dominance, *q.v.*

Pseudofertility. — The increase in fertility which sometimes results from pollination at the late bud stage in cases where, owing to incompatibility, such pollination would be ineffective or almost ineffective when carried out on the open flower.

Pseudogamy. — Diploid parthenogenesis in which the parthenogenetic egg develops into an organism. Often such development is stimulated by the presence of a male gamete but fertilization does not occur.

Pseudomitotic. — Diaschistic, *q.v.*

Pseudomixis. — Fusion between vegetative nuclei, or between cells which are not true gametes, leading to embryo formation.

Pseudo-reduction. — The halving of the chromosome number which appears to occur when pairing takes place.

Pseudova. — Parthenogenetic 'ova' capable of further development without fertilization.

Purebred. (Animal breeding). — An animal which is the descendant, in all lines of its ancestry, of individuals of the same type as itself (*cf*. WINTERS).

Pure Line. — A strain, the individual members of which are genetically pure as a result of continued in-breeding or self-fertilization or through other means.

Pycnosis. — A moribund nuclear condition in which all the chromosomes fuse in a single mass.

Pyridoxine. — Vitamin B_6.

Quadriplex. — Of a tetraploid having four doses of a specified dominant gene (AAAA).

Quadripolar Spindle. — A type of spindle with four poles found in sporocytes.

Quadrivalent. — An association of four chromosomes held together by chiasmata during the period from diplotene to metaphase of the first meiotic division.

Quadruplets. — Four individuals arising from a single birth whether monozygotic, dizygotic, or multizygotic

Quadruple Diploid. — An octoploid carrying in its somatic nuclei a double set of each of four specifically distinct genoms.

Quaternary Hybrid. — A hybrid derived from four grand-parental types all of which are different.

Quartet. — The four cells arising from a spore-mother cell

Quintuplets. — Five individuals arising from a single birth whether monozygotic or multizygotic.

R₂ Generation. — The progeny obtained by crossing a hybrid with one of its parents, a backcross progeny.

Rassenkreis — Rheogameon, *q v.*

Rate-gene. — A gene controlling the speed of any particular developmental process

Ratios. — *See* under Backcross Ratios, F_2 Ratios, Progeny Size and Appendix 1.

Ratoon. — A shoot from the base of the stem, or from the root, of a plant which has been cut back

Ray Floret. — One of the peripheral, typically uni-sexual, strap-like flowers arranged radially in a capitulum or other compact inflorescence.

Recapitulation. — The theory that the developmental stages of the individual's life-history recapitulate, in summarized form, the evolutionary life-history of the race; that is that ontogeny recapitulates phylogeny.

Receptive — Of a stigma, ripe for germinating pollen.

Recessive Character. — That one, of a pair of allelomorphic characters which will not appear when both allelic genes are present.

Reciprocal Chiasmata. — Chiasmata formed between two chromatids in such a way that a double crossing-over occurs in which the other two chromatids are not involved

Reciprocal Cross. — A second cross involving the same characters as the first but with the sexes of the parents interchanged.

Reciprocal Translocation. — Mutual translocation, a crossing over between non-homologous chromosomes

Recombination. — The rearrangement of linked genes due to crossing-over

Recombination Fraction. — The gametic output in a hybrid of new combinations of two genes expressed as a fraction or percentage of the total gametic output of new and old combinations combined. The formulae for the gametic output of the double heterozygote AaBb are (i) Coupling. ½(1 - p)AB, ½pAb, ½paB, ½(1 - p)ab; (ii) Repulsion: ½pAB,

½(1 - p)Ab, ½(1 - p)aB, ½pab, where p represents the recombination fraction Where there is no linkage, p = 0.5.

Recombination Index. — A measure of the mean number of independently segregating chromosome segments in the species, individual, etc. The recombination index is calculated by adding the gametic chromosome number to the average total number of chiasmata in the mother-cell

Recombination Value. — Recombination Fraction, *q.v.*

Recurrent Parent. — That parent of a hybrid with which it is again crossed or with which it is repeatedly crossed; the backcross parent.

Reduced Apogamy. — Haploid parthenogenesis. *See* under Parthenogenesis.

Reduced Fertilization. — Replacement of normal fertilization by the non-sexual union of cells, *e g.* by the union of two gametes both of the same sex (usually female).

Reduction. — (1) The halving of the chromosome number at meiosis. (ii) The relegation of a character to the immature stage of an animal (it being vestigial in the adult) although the character was present in both the young and adult stages of the animal's ancestors.

Reduction Division. — Reductional Division, *q v.*

Reductional Division. — A separation of homologous parts of chromosomes derived from opposite parents at anaphase of a first or second division (DARLINGTON). Heterotypic Division.

Reduplication. — The state of having one segment of a chromosome present twice in the one complement, the complement being otherwise undoubled.

Regression, Filial. — The tendency for the offspring of exceptional parents to revert towards the norm of the species.

Relationship Coefficient. — *See* Appendix 1.

Relaxin. — A sex hormone produced in the female reproductive glands of animals (including humans), which causes the symphysis pubis to relax thereby facilitating parturition.

Rensch's Rules (Birds). — (i) The races of a species which live in the cooler parts of the range of that species lay more eggs per clutch than the races in the warmer parts of the range. (ii) Stomach, intestines and caeca of birds that live on a mixed diet are relatively smaller in the tropical than in the temperate zone races. (iii) The wings of races that live in a cold climate or in the high mountains are relatively longer than those of the races which live in the lowlands or in a warm climate (MAYR, 1942).

Rensch's Rules (Mammals). — (i) The races in the warmer climates have less under fur and shorter contour hairs. (ii) The number of young in a litter averages higher in the cooler climates (MAYR, 1942).

Rensch's Rules (Snails). — (i) Land snails reach their greatest size in the area of optimum climate within the range of the species. (ii) The relative weight of the shell is highest in the forms exposed to the highest radiation of the sun (insolation) or to the greatest aridity. (iii) Land snails tend to have smooth glassy brown shells in cold climates, to have white or strongly sculptured shells in hot dry climates (MAYR, 1942).

Reproduction. — THOMAS (1940) classifies the various types of reproductive mechanism as shown in the table on the next page.

Reproductive Cell. — Gamete.

Repulsion. — Signifies that one recessive and one dominant allele are carried in one chromosome and that the two alternative dominant and recessive alleles are carried in the other chromosome. *See* under Recombination Fraction.

Residual Homology. — A degree of affinity still existing between once truly homologous chromosomes, which will now only rarely permit crossing-over between them (STEPHENS).

Resting Nucleus. — Any nucleus which is not undergoing division.

Resting Phase. — Interphase; the phase in the nuclear cycle when it is at rest in the sense of not dividing.

Restitution. — An induced chromosome break which has rejoined in the original way.

Restitution Nucleus. — A single nucleus formed through failure of the first division (ROSENBERG; DARLINGTON).

Restriction Factor. — A special form of modifying factor which reduces the effect of a particular major gene by limiting its phenotypic action to certain portions of the individual.

Retardation. — The slowing-down of the rate of action of a gene so that the character it controls is not affected till the late adult stage and thus becomes vestigial.

Reticulate. — Of evolution, species-formation, etc.: depending on repeated crossing between a number of lines. Reticulate evolution is characterized by the continual isolation of groups which are then again brought together so that diversity is increased by segregation and recombination.

Reverse Mutation. — The mutation of a mtuant gene back to its original state.

Types of Reproductive Mechanism:

General classification	Embryology	Special description	Genetical expectation
Embryo formed by fusion of nuclei or cells — Amphimixis	Fusion of pollen and egg nuclei	True sexual	Segregation
	Fusion of nuclei derived from the same mother cell — Automixis	Fusion of immediate products of meiosis	Segregation
		Fusion of haploid nuclei within the embryo sac	Segregation giving only homozygous progeny
Embryo not formed by fusion of nuclei or cells — Apomixis	Gametophyte formed — Embryo formed from diploid egg following non-reduction at meiosis	Diploid parthenogenesis	Segregation through crossing over
	Embryo formed from haploid egg following meiosis	Haploid parthenogenesis	Segregation
	Embryo formed from haploid nuclei other than egg	Apogamy	Segregation
	Gametophyte not formed — Embryo formed from diploid egg in embryo sac formed directly from somatic cell	Apospory	No segregation
	Embryo formed directly from nucellus	Nucellar embryony	Purely vegetative or clonal

Reversion. — The reappearance of an ancestral character not exhibited by the immediate parents and which has usually not appeared for several generations.

Rheogameon (Rassenkreis). — A species composed of segments of reasonably marked morphological divergence whose distributions are such that gene interchange may take place in sequence between them; individuals of contiguous segments are interfertile (CAMP & GILLY).

Riboflavine. — $C_{17}H_{20}O_6N_4$, one of the components of the vitamin B_2 complex.

Rings. — (i) At mitosis, chromosomes with no ends. (ii) At meiosis, chromosomes associated end to end in a ring, usually by terminal chiasmata; especially applied to diploid interchange heterozygotes where more than two chromosomes are so associated (DARLINGTON).

Rods. — Part of the Golgi apparatus.

Rogue. — N. A variation from the standard type of a variety or strain. V. To remove variant individuals from a variety, strain, etc.

Roguing. — The removal of undesirable individuals from a variety in the field.

Rose End. — The end of a tuber (typically a potato) furthest from the point of attachment. Most of the "eyes" (dormant buds) are at the rose end.

Rotation (of chiasmata). — The relative rotation of the four "arms" of a bivalent on either side of a chiasma, which often occurs between early diplotene and diakinesis (WHITE).

Rules, Ecological. — *See* under Allen, Bergmann, Gloger, Rensch.

Runner. — A procumbent shoot which takes root, forming a means of vegetative propagation.

Rut. — The period of sexual activity; oestrus.

S_1, S_2, S_3. — S_1: The immediate, self-bred, progeny of a plant (typically of a non-hybrid plant). S_2: the generation produced by sowing seed of an S_1. S_3: the progeny of an S_2, etc.

Salivary Gland Chromosomes. — Chromosomes in the nuclei of the salivary gland cells in *Diptera*. These chromosomes have undergone complete somatic pairing; consequently what is ordinarily called a salivary gland chromosome is thus really two chromosomes fused side by side (WHITE).

Salpingectomy. — A form of sterilization accomplished by cutting and ligature of the oviducts.

Saltant. — A new subdivision, type, or individual arising suddenly by mutation.

Saltation. — A discontinuous variation produced by mutation; a mutation.

Sarothrum. — Pollen-brush of insects.

SAT-chromosome. — A chromosome possessing one or more satellites, or a chromosome associated with the formation of the nucleolus; the letters SAT stand for 'sine acido thymonucleinico'.

Satellite. — A short segment of chromosome separated from the main body by one or more constrictions; trabant.

Saturation. — The complete absorption of the 'pairing-attraction' force of one chromosome by its homologous partner during pachytene pairing, as opposed to the absence of saturation at zygotene when several homologous chromosomes can be associated together as a multivalent.

S-bivalent. — A bivalent with a subterminal centromere.

Schizogenesis. — Reproduction by binary fission.

S-chromosome. — A chromosome with a sub-terminal centromere.

Scion. — The aerial portion of a plant, which is being propagated by grafting onto the rooted portion, or stock, of another plant.

Scopa. — The posterior metatarsal pollen brush of bees.

Scrub. — (i) An animal of mongrel breeding belonging to no definite type (ii) A low grade individual

Secondary Association. — The side-by-side association of bivalent chromosomes at meiosis

Secondary Kinetochore. — A secondary centre of attraction in addition to the normal centromere. *See* T-chromosome

Secondary Mutant. — Secondary trisomic. *See* Trisomic

Secondary Nucleus. — The nucleus resulting from the fusion of the two polar nuclei in the embryo-sac.

Secondary Pairing. — Secondary Association, *q v.*

Secondary Polyploid. — An allopolyploid in which some of the chromosomes in the basic set occur more frequently than others (CRANE & LAWRENCE)

Secondary Segregation. — The segregation in an allopolyploid of differences between its ultimate diploid parents (DARLING-TON).

Secondary Sexual Character. — A character without direct reproductive function whose expression is controlled by sex hormones

Sectional Hyperploidy. — The state of having one segment of a chromosome present both as part of the normal complement and, in addition, as a separate chromosome or as part of a non-homologous chromosome (as a result of transloca-tion) ; hyperdiploidy.

Sectorial Chimaera. — A plant with a deeply seated sector of genetically distinct tissue (CRANE & LAWRENCE)

Secundines. — (pl). The after-birth.

Seed, Elite. — Seed used for carrying on a special selected line from which stock seed will subsequently normally be produced Extra-pure seed.

Seed Generation (S G.). — S G. 1 represents the first seed generation i e. seed directly produced by cross-pollination and from which F_1 plants will grow, S G 2 represents self-bred seed from an F_1 — the second seed generation; S G 3, the third seed generation, is self-bred seed from an F_2, etc.

Seed, Stock. — Seed which is used by the seedsman to sow for the immediate production of commercial seed.

Segment. — Any given portion of a chromosome.

Segmental Interchange. — Mutual translocation; an exchange of non-homologous segments as between two chromosomes

Segmentation Nucleus. — The fused gametic nuclei in a zygote.

Segregation. — The separation of genes, or of chromosomes, of paternal and maternal origin at meiosis. *See* Secondary ——; Somatic ——.

Segregation, Effective. — That which gives viable gametic or zygotic combinations (especially following multiple association in structural hybrids) (DARLINGTON).

Selection. — The choosing of individuals with any specified desired characters from a population, with the object of improving or altering the average type. *See* Inter-specific Selection; Intra-Specific Selection; Intra-sexual Selection.

Selection, Darwin's Theory of Sexual. — DARWIN postulated: (i) that under certain circumstances there would occur a struggle between males for mates, and that the characters giving success in such a struggle would have sexually-selective value and would be perpetuated irrespective of their natural-selective value in the struggle for existence; (ii) that these characters would be of two main types, (*a*) those sub-serving male display, (*b*) those sub-serving combat between rival males. In addition DARWIN's theory postulates a rudimentary esthetic sense in females and a process of female choice as between rival males (*cf.* HUXLEY, 1938).

Selection, Epigamic. — Selection involving display characters common to both sexes (HUXLEY, 1938).

Selection, Intra-sexual. — All selection involving competition between individuals of one sex in the struggle for reproduction (HUXLEY, 1938).

Selective Fertilization. — A preferential fertilization in which certain types of gametes are more frequently fertilized than would be expected on a chance basis.

Selective Maturation. — Modified meiosis in which chromosomes derived from one parent go to one pole and those from the other parent to the other pole.

Self-bred. — Arising from an ovule, or ovules, fertilized by pollen from the same plant or from within the same clone.

Self-compatible. — Capable of fertilizing itself.

Self-fertilization. — The fertilization resulting from self-pollination.

Self-incompatible. — Incapable of self-fertilization.

Self-pollination. — Pollination between the pollen and stigmas of the same flower or within a clone.

Sematic Coloration. — Coloration promoting conspicuousness and used for warning or signalling purposes.

Semen. — The sperm-containing fluid ejaculated by male animals during coitus.

Semi-apospory. — The production of unreduced spores as a result of a pseudohomeotypic division (FAGERLIND).

Semi-dominance. — A reduced dominance characterized by the production of an intermediate phenotype in individuals heterozygous for the gene concerned, partial dominance.

Semi-heterotypic Division. — A first meiotic division which, through defective pairing, gives rise to a single nucleus—the 'restitution' nucleus.

Semi-lethal Factors. — *See* under Lethal Factors.

Seminal Vesicles. — Glands, located at the ends of the vasa deferentia, but connected, each by a duct, to the urethra. The seminal vesicles, at one time thought to act as a storage cavity for semen, secrete a fluid which is believed to provide a medium for transport of spermatozoa.

Sepal. — An individual segment of the calyx

Sepalody. — The production of sepal-like structures in place of petals.

Separation Theory, Wagner's. — The hypothesis that the formation of a real variety (DARWIN's "incipient species"), can succeed in nature only where some individuals can cross the previous borders of their range and segregate themselves for a long period from the other members of their species (*cf.* MAYR, 1942).

Septivalent. — *See* under univalent.

Serotinous. — Late flowering

Sertoli Cells. — The "nurse" cells to which the spermatids become attached whilst undergoing their development to spermia, which later become spermatozoa

Service Period. — The period between calving and subsequent conception.

Sesquidiploid. — A triploid produced by crossing a tetraploid species with a diploid species.

Set of Chromosomes. — The complement of chromosomes occurring in a gamete.

Sewal Wright Effect. — Non-adaptive differentiation into different types due to "drift" ($q v$) followed by random fixation in small isolated populations

Sex Chromosome. — A chromosome which has no truly similar homologue in the heterozygous sex and which is closely bound up with sex determination *See* W-, X-, Y-chromosomes

Sex Controlled Inheritance. — Sex-limited, *q.v.*

Sex Determination. — The genetic and allied phenomena which during ontogeny determine the sex of the adult organism.

Sex Glands. — Testes in the male and ovaries in the female.

Sex Hormones. — A group of hormones, belonging to the steroids, which affect or control the sexual organs and secondary sexual characters and manifestations.

Sex-index. — In insects (particularly *Drosophila*), the number of X-chromosomes per set of autosomes, *e.g.* a *Drosophila* male has a sex index of 0 5, a female is 1.0, a super-male 0.33 and a super-female 1.5.

Sex-influenced Factors. — Factors whose dominance is dependent on sex so that in one sex the heterozygote shows the character concerned whilst in the other sex the character is recessive.

Sex Limited. — The expression of a character in only one sex by reason of the essentially sexual nature of the character (*e g.* milk, eggs, horns in certain animals), or by reason of the gene responsible being unable to express itself on the genic background of one or other sex.

Sex Linkage. — The association which exists between sex and the hereditary factors borne on the sex chromosomes. *See* Partial Sex Linkage, Complete Sex Linkage.

Sex Linked Characters. — Hereditary characters whose genes are located on the sex chromosome

Sex Mosaic. — An organism showing attributes of both sexes; intersex.

Sex Ratio. — The number of males per hundred females, also given as the percentage of males in the total population or the percentage of males to total births.

Sex Reversal. — A change of the sexual nature of an individual from male to female or vice versa

Sex Transformation. — Sex reversal, *q v.*

Sexivalent. — *See* under Univalent.

Sexual Selection. — *See* under Selection, DARWIN's Theory of Sexual.

S.G. — Seed Generation, *q.v.*

S. Genes. — Genes controlling the specificity of incompatibility reactions in plants

Shift. — (i) The complete, permanent, masking of certain characters present in one of the original parents of an allotetraploid, due to regular homogenetic association of chromosomes in the allotetraploid Where such homogenetic pairing regularly occurs, any genes from one parent stock which are recessive to their homologues from the other parent stock will remain permanently masked. (ii) The removal of a segment of chromosome from one position and its inclusion in a new position on the same chromosome.

Short-day Plants. — Plants in which the commencement of flowering is speeded-up by a reduced period of daylight (normally less than twelve hours). Opp. Long-day Plants.

Sibbing. — Intercrossing brothers and sisters

Sibling, Sib. — One of two or more children of the same parents but not, necessarily, of the same birth.

Sibling Species. — Sympatric forms which are morphologically very similar or indistinguishable, but which possess specific biological characteristics and are reproductively isolated (MAYR, 1942).

Sibmating. — The crossing together of individuals of the same immediate parentage, *i e* the mating of brothers with sisters.

Silent Heat. — An oestrus cycle in which ovulation occurs but in which the outward signs of heat are lacking.

Silks. — The styles and stigmas in maize.

Simple Polyembryony. — Polyembryony brought about as a result of the formation of several eggs from a single megaspore.

Simplex. — (i) Heterozygous for a particular dominant gene. (ii) Of a tetraploid: having only one dose of a particular dominant gene (Aaaa).

Simplex-insufficient. — Used of duplicate genes to indicate that neither of them will, in the heterozygous state, give full expression to the character.

Simplex-sufficient. — Used of duplicate genes to indicate that either of them, in the heterozygous state, gives full expression to the character.

Single-dose Expression. — The degree of dominance or lack of dominance shown by a gene in the heterozygous state. Full single-dose expression is the equivalent of full dominance (true dominance), partial single-dose expression is partial dominance and absence of single-dose expression is the same as complete recessiveness.

Siphonogamy. — Fertilization when carried out by pollen tube.

Skein. — Spireme, *q.v.*

Slip. — A shoot, from the collar or lower part of the stem of a plant, used for propagation

S-M-C. — (i) Spermatocyte, or sperm mother-cell *See* under Spermatogonium (ii) Spore mother-cell, *q.v.*

Sobole. — A rhizome or underground creeping stem.

Somatic. — Pertaining to the body. Having two sets of chromosomes, one set normally coming from the male parent and the other from the female.

Somatic Doubling. — A doubling of the chromosome complement brought about as a result of an aberrant mitosis in which chromosome division takes place without nuclear division.

Somatic Mutation. — A mutation in a somatic cell, resulting in a chimaeral individual with respect to the mutant character (J. Heredity).

Somatic Pairing. — *See* under Pairing of Chromosomes.

Somatic Segregation. — The production of two genetically dissimilar cells at a somatic cell division, caused by some sudden qualitative or quantitative change in the nuclear constituents, or by the segregation of two dissimilar cytoplasmic constituents at the somatic cell divisions (CHITTENDEN).

Somatogenesis. — The study of the emergence under favourable surroundings of bodily form out of hereditary sources (WALTER).

Somatogenic Variations. — Environmentally produced variations, not heritable.

Somatoplastic Sterility. — The collapse of fertilized ovules during the early developmental stages (HAYES & IMMER).

Spay. — To destroy or excise the ovaries.

Spaying. — The castration of a female by removal or destruction of the ovaries.

Speciation. — The processes whereby new species are formed.

Speciation, Sympatric. — *See* Sympatric Speciation; Sympatric Speciation, Instantaneous.

Species. — Groups of actually or potentially interbreeding natural populations, which are reproductively isolated from other such groups (MAYR, 1942).

Specificity. — The degree of variation in the actual qualitative nature of the effect of a gene. Specificity is similar to expressivity but whereas the latter refers to the amount of effect caused by a gene, the former refers to the quality of that effect; clearly no hard and fast line can be drawn between specificity and expressivity.

Specific Modifiers. — Genes which modify the effect produced by other genes. They may be without effect themselves (FORD, 1945).

Speltoids. — A group of three types of wheat mutants which resemble *Triticum Spelta.*

Sperm. — The male gamete in animals. *See* under Spermatogonium.

Sperm-cell. — A male gamete.

Spermateleosis. — (i) The production of mature spermatozoa from spermatids (ii) Spermatogenesis.

Spermatid. — A haploid cell which develops directly into a functional sperm without further nuclear division. *See* under Spermatogonium.

Spermatoblast. — A spermatid, *q.v.*

Spermatocyte. — A sperm mother-cell. *See* under Spermatogonium.

Spermatogenesis. — The process by which spermatozoa are formed from spermatogonia

Spermatogonium. — A sperm mother-cell, a primordial male germ cell which by mitosis produces primary spermatocytes which in turn by meiosis produce secondary spermatocytes, these latter divide equationally to form spermatids which develop without further division into functional spermatozoa.

Spermatomere. — Sperm mother-cell

Spermatomerite. — A chromatin particle at the anterior end of a spermatozoon

Spermatoplasm. — The protoplasm of a spermatozoon.

Spermatosome. — The body of a spermatozoon as distinct from the chromosome content.

Spermatosphere. — Sperm mother-cell.

Spermatospore. — Sperm mother-cell.

Spermatozoid. — A motile male gamete in plants

Spermatozoon. — Sperm, *q.v.*

Spermin. — A testicular hormone affecting secondary sexual characters.

Spermiocalyptrotheca. — A cap-like structure forming the apex of a mature spermatozoon.

Spermiogenesis. — Spermatogenesis, *q v.*

Spermioteliosis. — Spermateleosis, *q v*

Sperm-nucleus. — The nucleus of a sperm, especially before fertilization after the sperm has penetrated an ovum.

Spermogamete. — Micro-gamete.

Sphere — Central Body, *q v.*

Spheroplasts. — Mitochondria, *q v.*

Spindle. — The frame-work of 'fibres', or striations which is formed between the two poles and the equatorial region, or between the two centrioles and the equatorial region, during cell division.

Spindle Attachment. — That point of a chromatid to which the spindle 'fibre' appears to be attached at metaphase and anaphase and which, at anaphase, starts to move towards the

pole before the rest of the chromatid; centromere; insertion
region; kinetochore.

Spindle Elements. — The 'fibres', striations or elements of
which a spindle is made up. *See* Spindle Fibres.

    Central Spindle Element. — A spindle element which is
not related to any of the chromosomes and which forms the
'core' of the spindle surrounded by the other elements which
lie parallel to it (WHITE).

Spindle Fibres. — Fibres which appear to connect the centromeres to the poles of the spindle during cell division. These
are possibly artefacts of fixation which correspond positionally
with some latent 'structure' of the spindle cytoplasm but which
do not exist as definite fibres until coagulated by chemical
reagents.

Spindle Spherule. — A specialized part of the centromere.

Spiral. — A coil of the chromosome thread (chromosome or
chromatid), at mitosis or meiosis. **Internal** ——, a coil within
a single chromatid between prophase and anaphase. **Relational**
——, coiling of two chromatids or chromosomes round one
another. **Major** ——, the larger internal coil at meiosis.
Minor ——, the smaller internal coil, **Relic** ——, the coiling
which survives at telophase and prophase. **Super** ——, larger
coils derived in prophase from the rearrangement of relic
spirals. **Molecular** ——, the coiling within the chromosome
thread which conditions internal and relational spirals (DAR-
LINGTON).

Spiral Cleavage. — A form of cell division which the fertilized
ovum undergoes in certain Annelida, Mollusca, Nemertina
and Platyhelmia in which the daughter cells are formed from
the old cells in certain regular positions which follow a
definite rule.

Spiralization. — The assumption of an internal (but not a
relational) spiral by the chromatids in mitosis and meiosis
(DARLINGTON).

Spireme. — (i) Prophase. (ii) The chromosomes during prophase.

Splitting. — Chromosomes are spoken of as 'split' when chromatid changes result from X-raying. The earliest stage when
chromatid changes are produced is called the 'beginning of
splitting'; the period when both chromatid and chromosome
changes occur together is called the 'duration of splitting';
'time of splitting' refers to the time when chromosome and
chromatid changes are produced equally often (Nomenclature
of NEWCOMBE, 1942).

Spontaneous Generation. — Abiogenesis, *q v.*

Spontaneous Univalent. — A chromosome which has remained unpaired at meiosis owing to the lack of a truly homologous partner. *cf.* Hereditary Univalent.

Spore. — A specialized cell usually produced by meiosis and capable of direct production of gametes.

Spore Mother-cell. — A diploid cell which divides meiotically to produce four haploid spores.

Sporocyte. — A spore mother-cell.

Sporogenesis. — Spore formation; the production of spores.

Sporogony. — Spore formation.

Sporophyte. — The spore producing individual in the higher plants. The sporophyte is the normal plant (with 2x chromosomes), it gives rise to the gametophyte (with x chromosomes) which produces the gametes.

Sporophytic Budding. — The production of an embryo from the tissue surrounding the embryo-sac.

Sporophytic Polyembryony. — Polyembryony brought about by the formation of adventitious embryos by budding from the nucellus or integument.

Sport. — A mutation, an abrupt deviation from type.

Spurious Pleiotropism. — See under Genuine Pleiotropism.

Stamen. — The male organ in the angiosperms, composed of an anther containing the pollen and a filament or stalk; the microsporophyll of the seed plants

Staminate. — Of flowers· bearing stamens only.

Staminode. — An abortive, or imperfectly developed, sterile stamen.

Staminodia. — Abortive sterile stamens.

Staminody. — The changing of floral parts into stamens.

Staminose. — Having stamens which are particularly obvious so that they form a marked feature of the flower.

Standard. — The large, upright petal at the back of a papilionaceous flower.

Standard Deviation. — *See* Appendix 1

Standardised Fertility. — The crude birth rate corrected by a statistical method intended to make allowance for changes in age composition in the population (CARPENTER).

Stasimorphy. — Alteration in form caused by arrested development.

Stathmokinesis. — Complete inhibition of anaphase and cell division by treatment with colchicine or some other aberration-inducing substance.

Staurigamia. — Cross fertilization.

Stem Body. — The equatorial portion of the spindle-cytoplasm between the two groups of daughter chromosomes at late anaphase, which, by elongating, helps to separate the two groups of chromosomes more widely.

Stenoplastic. — Having little or no modificational plasticity, *q.v.* N. **Stenoplasty.**

Stenotribal. — Of, or pertaining to, flowers whose anthers are so arranged as to dust their pollen on the under part of the thorax of their insect visitors (CARPENTER).

Step Allelomorphism. — The theory that the locus of one gene may contain a group of sub-genes arranged in linear order and each contributing its definite and characteristic quota to the phenotype. Each such sub-gene would be only partially allelomorphic to the other sub-genes within the one gene locus. *cf.* Fractionation.

Stereoplasm. — The more viscous portion of the protoplasm.

Stigma. — That portion of the style which is adapted for receiving pollen.

Stigmasterol. — A steroid from soya beans used in the synthesis of progesterone and testosterone for clinical use.

Stilboestrol, — dipropionate. — *See* Oestrogens.

Stock. — The rooted plant onto which a graft is made.

Stolon. — A runner, or creeping stem capable of forming adventitious roots and acting as a means of vegetative propagation. Adj. **Stoloniferous.**

Strain. — A group within a variety which constantly differs in one or more genetic factors from the variety proper.

Strepsitene. — Late diplotene when the successive loops between chiasmata coming to lie at right angles give the appearance of merely twisting round one another; a misnomer (DIXON; DARLINGTON).

Structure. — The linear arrangement of the genes in the chromosomes.

Structural Change. — Change in the genetic structure of the chromosome. May be intra-radial or extra-radial with respect to arms, internal, fraternal or external with regard to chromosomes, symmetrical or asymmetrical with respect to the possession of a centromere, eucentric or dyscentric with respect to the direction of a segment in relation to the centromere. **Secondary—— ——,** is change in structure resulting from crossing-over between two homologous segments in chromosomes which are structurally different on both sides of these segments (DARLINGTON).

Structural Heterozygote. — Structural Hybrid, *q.v.*

Structural Hybrid. — One whose parental gametes differed in respect of the structure of their chromosomes. It is **Eucentric** when its dislocated segments have the same linear sequence with respect to the centromere, **Dyscentric** when they are relatively inverted (DARLINGTON).

Style. — An elongated part of the carpel between the ovary and stigma.

Sub-gene. — *See* under Step Allelomorphism.

Sub-lethal. — Semi-lethal. *See* Lethal Factors.

Subsexual Reproduction. — Parthenogenesis following ameiosis with non-reduction, but with segregation owing to crossing-over (DARLINGTON).

Subspecies. — "The subspecies, or geographic race (*q.v.*), is a geographically localized subdivision of the species, which differs genetically and taxonomically from other subdivisions of the species" (MAYR, 1942).

Succession. — The lagging of the sex chromosomes behind the autosomes in passing to the poles after meiosis.

Succession, Law of. — The hypothesis that every species has come into existence coincident, both in time and space, with a pre-existing and closely allied species.

Successional Speciation. — The gradual evolution of new species from old over a long period of time. The characteristic of this form of speciation is that a given type gradually changes so that forms meriting new specific names eventually emerge, later, differences of sufficient magnitude may arise to necessitate new generic names.

Superfemale. — A *Drosophila* fly or other insect having three X chromosomes per double set of autosomes.

Superfetation. — Superfoetation, *q.v.*

Superfoetation. — Fertilization of a second ovum in a pregnant animal after a considerable interval from the original conception; hypercyesis.

Supermale. — A *Drosophila* fly or other insect having a single X-chromosome per double set of autosomes. *See* Supersexes.

Supernumeraries. — Inert chromosomes present in some, but not in all, the members of a species.

Super-reduction. — The production of pollen grains or ovules with half, or approximately half, the normal gametic number of chromosomes as a result of irregularities in nuclear division.

Supersexes. — Individuals in the *Insecta* with an abnormal ratio of X-chromosomes to sets of autosomes. *See* Superfemale and Supermale.

Superspecies. — A monophyletic group of geographically representative (allopatric) species which are morphologically too distinct to be included in one species (MAYR, 1942).

Supplementary Factors. — Factors which by themselves have no effect but which qualitatively alter the effect of another factor; modifying factors.

Suppressor. — Any gene which, either in the heterozygous or homozygous state, nullifies the effect of a major gene but which, by itself, has no effect.

Suppressor Mutation — A sudden change occurring at a particular chromosomal locus such that a gene is formed capable of nullifying the effect of a particular major gene.

Surculigerous. — Reproducing by suckers.

Surculose. — Producing suckers which give rise to independent plants.

Surculus. — A sucker.

Survival of the Fittest. — The corollary of the theory of Natural Selection namely that, as a result of the elimination by natural selection of those individuals least suited to the environment, those which ultimately remain are the fittest.

Switch Genes. — Genes which cause certain regions of developing tissue to take an abnormal choice out of a range of alternative possible paths (WADDINGTON).

Symmetrical Chiasmata. — Chiasmata which are either reciprocal (*q.v.*) or complementary (*q.v.*); comparate chiasmata. Opp. Dispaiate Chiasmata.

Sympatric. — Inhabiting one and the same area.

Sympatric Hybridization. — The production of a hybrid between two good species that coexist over wide parts of their ranges without mixing (MAYR, 1942).

Sympatric Speciation. — Reproductive isolation and speciation which takes place within a single local population. This can occur either instantaneously (*q.v.*) or by ecological specialization (*cf.* MAYR, 1942).

Sympatric Speciation, Instantaneous. — The pioduction of a single individual (or the offspring of a single mating) which is reproductively isolated from the species to which the parental stock belongs (MAYR, 1942).

Sympetalous. — With petals united to form a tube, gamopetalous.

Symplast. — Coenocyte, *q v.*

Synacme. — The simultaneous maturation of pollen and stigmas.

Synantherous. — With anthers joined to form a tube.

Synanthesis. — Simultaneous maturation of stamens and stigmas

Synaposematism. — Mullerian mimicry Adj. **Synaposematic.**

Synapsis. — (1) Syndesis, the pairing of homologous chromosomes of maternal and paternal origin in the prophase of meiosis. (11) Synizesis, the contraction figure which often appears at this stage in which the chromatin appears to be massed to one side of the nucleus.

Synaptene. — Zygotene, the stage in the prophase of meiosis during which homologous chromosomes come together in pairs.

Synchronic Species. — Species which belong to the same time level.

Synchronous Mitosis. — The occurrence of a number of cell divisions which take place at exactly the same time in a group of neighbouring cells (WHITE)

Syncryptic. — Resemblance of different species to a common environmental background due to cryptive adaptation.

Syncytium. — A multi-nucleate protoplasmic agglomeration arising as a result of cell fusion cf Coenocyte.

Syndesis. — Association of homologous chromosomes during meiosis.

Syndiploidy. — The doubling of the chromosome number through failures in the mitotic spindle. Such a doubling, when it occurs in germinal tissue prior to meiosis may give rise to diploid gametes

Syndrome, Genetic. — A genetically controlled group of symptoms occurring together.

Syngameon. — A habitually interbreeding community of individuals (LOTSY, 1931).

Syngamy. — Union of gametes in fertilization.

Syngenesious. — Having the anthers united (as in *Compositae*).

Syngenesis. — (i) Sexual reproduction. (11) The state of having direct or common descent from the same ancestors; blood relationship.

Syngenetic Relations. — Blood relations; individuals which have direct or common descent from the same ancestors.

Synheterosis. — The stimulus causing hybrid vigour in diploid organisms (DODGE)

Synizesis. — *See* under Synapsis

Synkaryon. — A zygote-nucleus, a nucleus resulting from the conjugation of two nuclei.

Synoecious. — Having staminate and pistillate flowers both present in the same head

Synspermous. — Having the seeds fused together. N **Synspermy.**

Syntechny. — Similarity due to a common environment. Adj. **Syntechnic.**

Synthetic Variety. — A term used particularly with cross-pollinated plants to refer to a variety produced by the combination of selected lines of plants and subsequent normal pollination (HAYES & IMMER)

Systemic Mutation. — *See* under Macro-evolution

T-chromosome. — A chromosome which in addition to the usual centromere, has a secondary centre of attraction towards the pole. Where this secondary centre is located at the end of a chromosome, the term **T-end** is used. These secondary centres do not appear to be translocated centromeres (*cf.* ÖSTERGREN and PRAKKEN).

T-effect. — Any phenomenon associated specifically with the secondary attraction centres found in T-chromosomes, *q v.* T-bivalents, T-rods, T-trivalents refer to bivalents, rods, etc showing the T-effect.

T-end. — *See* under T-chromosome.

Tachyauxesis. — Ontogenetic heterauxesis in which the growth of the part is faster than that of the body as a whole.

Tachygenesis. — An abbreviated, quickened development in which one or more of the embryonic or larval developmental stages are omitted.

Tachytelic. — Evolving much faster than the modal rate *cf.* Horotelic and Bradytelic.

Tandem Satellites. — Two short segments of chromosome separated from each other by a constriction and from the main body of the chromosome by a second constriction.

Tassel. — The staminate inflorescence of maize.

Telegony. — The erroneously supposed influence of one mate of a female on her progeny by other subsequent mates.

Teleianthous. — Of a flower· complete, hermaphrodite

Teleology. — The doctrine that evolution is purposive with a definite goal and that biological structures can be interpreted in terms of the purpose they serve. Adj. **Teleological.**

Teleosis. — Evolution by teleology, *q v.* Adj. **Telic.**

Telianthous. — Teleianthous, *q v.*

Telocentric Chromosome. — A chromosome with a terminal centromere.

Telokinesis. — Telophase, *q v.*

Telolecithal. — Of an egg· having the bulk of the yolk in one hemisphere.

Telomere. — (i) A gene situated at the end of a chromosome. (ii) A chromosome end.

Telomitic. — (Of chromosomes) with terminally attached spindle fibres; having the centromere terminal.

Telophase. — The last stage in cell division before the nucleus returns to the resting phase. *See* Mitosis; Meiosis.

Telosynapsis. — The end-to-end association of chromosomes sometimes seen at zygotene; telosyndesis.

Telosyndesis. — Telosynapsis, *q.v.*

Teratism. — Morphological or anatomical abnormality.

Teratology. — The study of morphological or anatomical abnormalities (especially malformations or monstrosities).

Terminal Affinity. — The property by which chromosomes are held together end to end from diplotene till metaphase or brought together in this way at metaphase (DARLINGTON).

Terminal Chiasma. — A chiasma, or physical exchange of partners, which occurs at the extremity of the chromatids.

Terminal Gene. — A gene situated at the extreme end of a chromosome; telomere.

Terminal Granules. — Granular bodies which occur at the ends of some of the chromosomes in certain plant species. These granules should not be confused with satellites.

Terminal Trabant. — *See* Trabant.

Terminalization. — Expansion of the association of the two pairs of chromatids on one side of a chiasma at the expense of that on the other side. So called because the resulting "movement" of the chiasma is usually, if not always, towards the ends of chromosomes. **Arrest of** ——. Stoppage of the movement of a chiasma, through the opposite segments distal to it being non-homologous (DARLINGTON).

Terminalization Coefficient. — The number of terminal chiasmata divided by the total number of chiasmata.

Territoriality. — Persistent attachment to a specific small territory.

Tertiary Mutant. — A tertiary trisomic. *See* Trisomic.

Tertiary Split. — Longitudinal doubleness of the chromonema of each chromatid which may become visible during the first or second division of meiosis.

Testcross. — A cross between a heterozygote and a recessive homozygote.

Tester Strain. — A strain whose genetic make-up is such that its contribution to the inheritance of the offspring will not hide

the inheritance being received from the parent being progeny-tested (*cf.* LUSH, 1943).

Testicle, Testis. — A male gonad; an organ within which spermatozoa are formed.

Testosterone, — acetate, — dipropionate, — propionate. Testosterone is believed to be the hormone secreted by the testis and responsible for the growth of the secondary sex glands in the male (ROBSON). *See* Androgens

Tetrabasic. — Comprising four univalents.

Tetracyte — One of the four daughter cells formed by meiosis from a mother cell.

Tetrad. — (i) A group of four cells formed meiotically, *e.g.* pollen tetrad. (ii) Four chromatids which together comprise a bivalent at meiosis.

Tetrad Divisions. — The first and second meiotic divisions which the spore mother-cell undergoes to form four spores.

Tetragenic. — Controlled by four genes

Tetraplant. — Tetraploid.

Tetraploid. — Having four haploid sets of chromosomes in its somatic cells; an organism of this type.

Tetrasomaty. — The production of somatic nuclei with four times the normal somatic chromosome number; octoploidy.

Tetrasome. — An association of four homologous chromosomes at meiosis.

Tetrasomic. — An organism having one of its chromosomes present four times in each somatic nucleus, the other chromosomes being present only twice, *i e* 2x + 2.

Tetraster. — Used of cell division when a spindle mechanism is formed having four poles.

Thalamus. — The receptacle of a flower.

Thanatosis. — A form of mimicry in which death is feigned.

Theca. — A sheath covering an organ, particularly the layer of ovarian connective-tissue stroma surrounding a Graafian follicle

Theelin. — A female sex hormone.

Theelol. — A female sex hormone.

Thelygenic. — Producing offspring consisting entirely, or almost entirely, of females. N. **Thelygeny.**

Thelykaryon. — The nucleus of a female gamete.

Thelyplasm. Female cell-plasm as distinct from male protoplasm or arrhenoplasm.

Thelytoky. — Parthenogenesis in which females only are produced.

Thelytonic. — Parthenogenetic.

Thermocleistogamy. — Self pollination taking place within flowers the opening of whose perianth has been inhibited by low temperature.

Thiamin, Thiamine. — Aneurine; vitamin B_1 ($C_{12}H_{18}N_4$ $SOCl_2$), the anti-neuritic vitamin.

Thixotropy. — The property of liquefying when agitated and of returning to the 'gel' condition on standing. This property is shown by some colloids. Adj. **Thixotropic.**

Three-breed Crossing. — A system of breeding in which breed A is crossed with B and the F_1 with C, this hybrid is then crossed with B and the product is crossed with A to produce a hybrid which is crossed with C; the next cross is with B and then A and so on.

Three-way Cross. — A cross between an F_1 and another variety so that three parental types enter into the resulting hybrid.

Thremmatology. — Plant and animal breeding for domestic uses.

Throwing-back. — The reappearance of a character after a lapse of one or more generations due to the character being recessive or being dependent on complementary factors, or as a result of back-mutation; atavism. Such an aberrant individual is called a throw-back.

Thrum-eyed. — Having the anthers at the throat of the corolla and the stigma below, enclosed within the corolla-tube.

Tocopherol. — A group of alcohols which show vitamin E activity. α-Tocopherol, $C_{29}H_{50}O_2$, and β-tocopherol, $C_{28}H_{48}O_2$, have been isolated from wheat-germ-oil and γ-tocopherol occurs in cotton seed oil.

Top-cross. — Inbred-variety cross, *q.v.*

Topoclines. — Geoclines (*q.v.*), particularly where the distances involved are very great.

Torsion-pairing. — Non-homologous association at pachytene which releases a torsion without satisfying an attraction (DARLINGTON).

Trabant. — A short segment of chromosome separated from the main body of the chromosome by one or more constrictions. An **intercalary trabant** has a constriction at each end, whereas a **terminal trabant** being situated at the end of a chromosome has but one constriction. A **lateral trabant** has only one constriction but is itself a branch of the chromosome proper.

Tractile Fibre. — A 'fibre' connecting the centromere with the pole at cell division.

Transgenation. — A heritable change taking place at a single gene locus, presumably caused by chemical alteration of the individual gene; a mutation proper, point-mutation or geno-variation

Transgressive Segregation. — The appearance in the F_2 (or later) generation of a cross of individuals showing a more extreme development of a character than either parent (J. Heredity).

Transient Polymorphism. — *See* under Polymorphism

Translocation. — The shifting of a segment of a chromosome to another part of the same chromosome, or the attachment of a fragment of one chromosome to a non-homologous chromosome.

Traumatin. — $C_{11}H_{17}O_4N$; a plant wound-hormone which stimulates cell division. *cf.* Allantoin.

Triad. — Three daughter cells arising (instead of a tetrad) from a spore mother-cell, as a result of meiotic irregularities.

Triaster. — Used of cell division when a spindle mechanism is formed having three poles

Tribe. — A combination of one or more families, the foundresses of which trace in the female line to a common ancestress which is the foundress of the tribe (WINTERS).

Trichlamydeous. — Of a periclinal chimaera (*q v.*): having the genetically distinct peripheral tissue three layers of cells thick.

Trigamous. — Having pistillate, perfect and staminate flowers all present in the one head.

Trigeneric Hybrid. — An individual produced by crossing two distinct genera and crossing the F_1 with a third genus

Trigenic. — Controlled by three genes.

Trigynous. — Three styled

Triheterozygote. — An organism heterozygous for three genes

Trihybrid. — A hybrid resulting from a cross between parents differing in three genes.

Trimonoecious. — Having perfect, staminate and pistillate flowers on the one plant.

Trimorphism. — The occurrence of three distinct forms within a species. *See* Polymorphism.

Trioecious. — Having perfect, staminate and pistillate flowers on different individual plants within the species.

Triphenyl Chloro-ethylene. — *See* under Oestrogens.

Triple Fusion. — The fusion between the two polar nuclei and a male gamete, which takes place in the embryo-sac and which gives rise to the endosperm.

Triplex. — A tetraploid zygote in which a particular dominant gene is represented three times (AAAa).

Triplicate Genes. — Three, non-cumulative, identical, but non-allelic genes.

Triplo-. — The term triplo-, folowed by a symbol designating a particular chromosome, indicates an individual in whose somatic cells there are three members of this particular chromosome. *cf.* Haplo-; Diplo-.

Triploid. — Having three haploid sets of chromosomes in the somatic cells.

Trisomic. — An organism with three chromosomes of one type; usually otherwise diploid ($2x + 1$). A diploid organism is said to be doubly trisomic, not tetrasomic, when it has the two extra chromosomes of two different types ($2x + 1 + 1$) (DARLINGTON). **Secondary** ——. A trisomic organism in which the extra chromosome has two identical ends. **Tertiary** ——. A trisomic organism in which the extra chromosome is made up of halves corresponding with the halves of different chromosomes in the normal set (BELLING; DARLINGTON).

Trisomy. — The state of having one, or more, chromosomes present three times in the somatic cells, the other chromosomes being present only twice.

Trivalent. — An association of three chromosomes held together by chiasmata between the diplotene stage and metaphase of the first meiotic division.

Trophic Nucleus. — The larger of two nuclei in a cell; vegetative nucleus; macronucleus; trophonucleus.

Trophochromatin. — Chromatin which governs the nutritive functions of the cell.

Trophochromidia. — Chromidia which are mainly concerned with the nutritive functions of the cell.

Trophonucleus. — The larger or 'vegetative' nucleus in certain *Protozoa*.

Trophoplasm. — 'Vegetative' or nutritive protoplasm. Unmodified cytoplasm as distinct from kinoplasm.

Trophoplast. — Plastid, *q.v.*

Tropokinesis. — Rotation of the spindle axis, usually as a result of treatment with colchicine or some other aberration-inducing substance.

Tube Nucleus. — The nucleus which occurs in any growing pollen tube and which does not take part in fertilization but is concerned with regulating the growth and behaviour of the tube.

Tuber. — A fleshy underground stem specialized for food storage and capable of giving rise to a new plant.

Tunica albuginea. — (i) The outer sheath of dense fibrous tissue surrounding the central core of a testis. (ii) A fibrous layer surrounding the ovary.

Unbalance. — *See* Balance

Unconditioned Reflex. — Hereditarily determined reflex actions which appear in all normal members of the species and which do not result from individual experience or habit. *cf.* Conditioned Reflex.

Unequal Bivalent. — A bivalent in which one of the constituent chromosomes is longer than the other, so that it has **an** unpaired region at one end (WHITE) *See* Univalent.

Uniovular Twins. — Monozygotic twins; twins arising from a single egg.

Uniparous. — Producing only one offspring at a birth.

Unipolar Spindle. — A type of spindle with only one pole which occurs during meiosis in some insects, a 'half-spindle.'

Unisexual. — Of one sex, *i.e.* male or female, as opposed to hermaphrodite

Unisexualism. — The state of having the two sexes separated by reason of their being confined to separate individuals

Unit Character. — In mendelian inheritance, a character or alternative difference of any kind, which is either present or absent, as a whole, in each individual, and which is capable of becoming associated in new combinations with other unit characters (HAYES & GARBER).

Univalent. — A body at the first meiotic division corresponding with a single chromosome in the complement, especially when unpaired Bivalent, Trivalent, Quadrivalent, Quinquevalent, Sexivalent, Septivalent, Octavalent (for Octovalent), etc are associations of chromosomes held together between diplotene and metaphase of the first division by chiasmata. Similar associations of more than two including non-homologous chromosomes in structural hybrids should be described as "unequal bivalents", "associations" or "rings" of three, four, etc. (*see* Hexad). The hybrid forms, "monovalent", "tetravalent", "pentavalent", "hexavalent", etc, used in chemistry should be avoided (DARLINGTON).

Unmatched S Gene. — Any S gene which is represented either
in the style or pollen but not in both, in a given pollination
(LEWIS). (An S gene is any gene controlling the specificity
of incompatibility reactions in plants).

Unreduced Apogamy. — Euapogamy; the development of a
sporophyte direct from a gametophyte without fertilization
having taken place so that no zygote is formed *See* Parthenogenesis.

Uterus. — The organ in which the mammalian foetus is carried
during pregnancy.

Uterus Masculinus. — A small structure lying between the
ejaculatory ducts of the male and homologous with the uterus
of the female; 'organ of Weber'.

Vagina. — The canal leading from the uterus to the external genital opening in female mammals.

Vagina, Artificial. — A double walled rubber tube to which is fitted at one end, a glass receptacle and which is used in artificial insemination in collecting semen from the male. The space between the double walls is usually filled with warm water.

Variance. — (σ^2). The mean squared deviation from the mean: $\sigma^2 = \dfrac{S(d^2)}{n-1}$ where d is the difference between an observation and the mean, n is the total number of observations and S represents summation over all the squares of the differences.

Variant. — An organism differing slightly from the type.

Variations. — The differences between the individuals in any given related population.

Variegation. — Spots or patches of different colour; generally a mosaic or chimaera but sometimes caused by disease or other environmental factors.

Variety. — A group of strains or a single strain which, by its structural or functional characters, can be differentiated from another group.

Vasa deferentia. — A continuation of the epididymi lying between these and the urethra. In some animals each vasa deferens has an enlargement (the ampulla of Henle) which functions as a storage place for spermatozoa

Vasectomy. — A form of sterilization accomplished by the removal (or ligature) of a small section of each spermatic duct.

V-chromosomes. — Chromosomes with two arms, *i.e.* mediocentric chromosomes

Vegetative Apogamy. — The production of a sporophyte directly from the vegetative cells of the gametophyte without any sexual act.

Vegetative Nucleus. — (i) The larger of two nuclei in a cell; macronucleus; trophic nucleus; trophonucleus. (ii) Pollen tube-nucleus.

Vegetative Pole. — The lower portion of a telolecithal ovum in which the yolk accumulates

Vegetative Reproduction. — Asexual reproduction by buds, grafts, cuttings, layers, etc

Vegetative Segregation. — The production of two genetically dissimilar cells at a somatic cell division, caused by some sudden qualitative or quantitative change in the nuclear constituents, or by the segregation of two dissimilar cytoplasmic constituents at the somatic cell divisions (CHITTENDEN)

Veratrine Sulphate. — Veratrine, a poisonous alkaloid, is obtained from dried ripe seeds of *Shoenocaulon officinale* and from rhizomes of *Veratrum album* and *V. viride.* The sulphate is used in inducing polyploidy

Vernalization. — The treatment of seeds, before sowing, by any technique designed to hasten the flowering period of the plants to which the seeds give rise.

Versatile Anthers. — Those having the filament attached near the middle, so that the anther can readily turn in any direction

Viable. — Capable of living more or less normally, capable of germinating normally.

Vicinism. — Out-crossing; natural cross-pollination.

Vicinist. — A plant resulting from vicinism; a natural hybrid.

Virgin Birth. — *See* Apogamy; Apomixis; Parthenogenesis.

Vitamer. — One of two or more substances which have a similar capacity for curing any specific deficiency syndrome.

Vitamin. — A vitamin is a substance with a catalytic action which is indispensable to animals. Since it cannot be synthesized by animals and must be furnished by plants, its origin is exogenous as far as animals are concerned. (SCHOPFER).

Vitamin A. — The fat-soluble vitamin controlling night-blindness and the disease resisting power of mucous membranes. Vitamin A is manufactured by the liver from carotene, *q v.*

Vitamin B$_1$. — $C_{12}H_{18}N_4SOCl_2$. The water-soluble, heat labile, anti-neuritic vitamin controlling beri-beri, aneurin; aneurine, thiamin; thiamine.

Vitamin B$_2$. — The water soluble, heat stable, anti-pellagra vitamin complex which contains amongst other substances riboflavine and nicotinic acid, *q.v.*

Vitamin C. — $C_6H_8O_6$ The water-soluble, readily-oxidisable, anti-scorbutic vitamin, ascorbic acid, hexuronic acid.

Vitamin D. — The anti-rachitic, fat-soluble vitamin. *See* Calciferol and 7-Dehydrocholesterol.

Vitamin E. — The reproductive, fat-soluble vitamin It is resistant to heat. light and oxidation. *See* Tocopherol.

Vitamin G. — Vitamin B_2, *q v*

Vitamin K. — This controls the coagulating power of blood. Its composition is possibly 2 methyl-3-hydroxy-1:4 naphthoquinone.

Vitamin P. — A flavone derivative concerned with permeability, citrin.

Vitelline Body. — Yolk nucleus, *q v.*

Vivipary. — (1) The replacement of the floral structures by a vegetative outgrowth capable of developing into a new plant. (ii) Giving birth to living offspring (as opposed to laying eggs from which living offspring subsequently hatch).

Von Baer's Laws. — (i) In development from the egg the general characters appear before the special characters. (ii) From the more general characters the less general and finally the special characters are developed. (iii) During its development an animal departs more and more from the form of other animals (iv) The young stages in the development of an animal are not like the adult stages of other animals lower down on the scale, but are like the young stages of those animals (DE BEER),

W-chromosomes. — The sex chromosomes in moths, caddis flies, birds and certain fishes. In these types the male has two similar heterosomes (ZZ) and the female has two dissimilar one (ZW). In some cases the female is Z only, with no W homologue

Waagen, Mutations of. — Discontinuous changes of small or moderate extent, particularly used of different forms of fossils of the same lineage but belonging to different horizons.

Wagner's Separation Theory. — *See* Separation Theory, Wagner's

Warning Coloration. — Conspicuous coloration (especially red) of obnoxious organisms, particularly insects.

Weber, Organ of. — The uterus masculinus, a small structure lying between the ejaculatory ducts of the male and homologous with the uterus of the female.

Weissmannism. — Essentially a theory of complete continuity of germ-plasm from generation to generation, this remaining entirely distinct from somatoplasm.

Wings. — The lateral petals of a papilionaceous flower.

Wright's Coefficient. — *See* under Inbreeding Coefficient, Appendix 1.

Wright, Sewall, Effect. — Non-adaptive differentiation into different types due to "drift" (*q.v.*) followed by random fixation in small isolated populations.

x. — The basic number of chromosomes in a polyploid series.

X_1, X_2, X_3. — First, second and third generations following irradiation with X-rays.

X-chromosome. — The sex chromosome which is associated with an identical homologue in one sex (the homozygous sex) and with a dissimilar partner in the other sex. In most animals the homozygous sex is the female (XX) the male being XY Some biologists reserve X and Y for this relationship using W and Z for the heterosomes where the homozygous sex is the male (*see* W-chromosomes). The X-chromosome may be unpaired in certain organisms *See* Compound X-chromosomes.

Xenia. — The effect of pollen on the embryonic and maternal tissues of a fruit. (Some writers limit xenia to effects on embryo and endosperm using the term **metaxenia** for any effects produced by pollen on maternal tissues of the fruit).

Xenogamy. — Cross-pollination within a species.

Xenoplastic Graft. — A heteroplastic graft (*i.e.* an inter-specific or inter-generic graft) which "takes" successfully.

Xerocleistogamy. — Self pollination taking place within flowers whose perianths have been prevented from opening by excessive dryness.

Yarovization. — Vernalization; the treatment of seeds, before sowing, by any technique designed to hasten the onset of the flowering period of the plants to which the seeds give rise.

Y-chromosome. — The sex chromosome which is paired with a dissimilar partner in one sex (the heterozygous sex), and which is absent in the other sex (the homozygous sex). *See* X-chromosome.

Yolk Nucleus. — Vitelline body; a cytoplasmic body in the young oocyte, which serves as a centre for the yolk-formation in many forms. In many cases it is traceable to the idiozome and its associated structures (CARUS; WILSON).

Z-chromosomes. — *See* W-chromosomes; X-chromosomes.

Zoidiophily. — Pollination by means of animals

Zoogamete. — A motile gamete

Zoogamy. — Sexual procreation in animals

Zoogonous. — Viviparous, giving birth direct to live young, as opposed to the production of eggs.

Zoogony. — Vivipary.

Zoophily. — Pollination by animals.

Zygonema. — The chromosome thread during the zygotene phase, when the chromosomes have come together in pairs.

Zygosis. — Conjugation.

Zygosome. — A newly fused chromosome pair produced by syndesis (zygotene), mixochromosome.

Zygotaxis. — Attraction as between gametes of opposite sex.

Zygote. — The cell which results from gametic fertilization and, by extension, the individual which eventually grows from this cell

Zygotene. — (i) The stage in the prophase of meiosis during which homologous chromosomes come together in pairs. (ii) The paired chromosome threads at this stage.

Zygotic Incompatibility. — A form of homomorphic incompatibility (*q.v.*) in which the incompatibility reaction depends directly on the genetic constitution of the zygote producing the male gamete, rather than that of the male gamete itself, together with the constitution of the female zygote. (cf. MATHER). *cf* Gametic Incompatibility.

Zygotic Lethal. — A lethal factor whose effect is only apparent in the embryo, larva or adult as distinct from a **Gametic Lethal** which renders inviable any gamete which carries it.

Zygotic Meiosis. — Meiosis which takes place in the first two divisions after fertilization, at the beginning of the life cycle of an organism; initial meiosis; zygotic reduction.

Zygotic Mutation. — A mutation occurring in the zygote shortly after fertilization.

Zygotic Number. — The somatic (2n) chromosome number as opposed to the haploid or gametic (n) number

Zygotic Reduction. — Meiosis when it takes place immediately after fertilization, zygotic meiosis.

Zygotic Sterility. — Sterility due to the production of gametes which form inviable zygotes; diplontic sterility

APPENDICES

Appendix 1

Useful Formulae

Chi (χ):

$$\chi^2 = S\left(\frac{a^2}{e}\right) - n$$

where a and e are the observed and expected numbers respectively in any class, n is the total number of individuals in all classes and S stands for summation over all classes For two-class ratios with an expectation of y 1

$$\chi^2 = \frac{(b - yc)^2}{y(b + c)}$$

where b and c are the actual numbers observed in the two classes.

Correlation Coefficient. (r) .

$$r = \frac{S(dx \cdot dy)}{\sqrt{Sdx^2 \ Sdy^2}}$$

$dx =$ the deviation of the individual x variables from the mean of x

$dy =$ the deviation of the individual y variables from the mean of y

S stands for summation over all classes

Genotypes, Number of. — The number of distinct genotypes expected in F_2 is given by calculating 3^n where n is the number of factor-pairs involved. In a backcross the number of genotypes would be 2^n.

Homozygotes, Proportion of. — The percentage of homozygous individuals in a progeny is given by calculating

$$\left(\frac{2^a - 1}{2^a}\right)^n \times 100$$

where a is the number of generations of selfing or backcrossing and n is the number of heterozygous genes. In selfing, following crossing, this formula gives the percentage of homozygous individuals in any one generation, but these individuals will belong to a number of different genotypes In backcrossing, this formula gives the percentage of homozygous individuals, in any one generation, belonging to the backcross-parent (recurrent-parent) genotype as regards the n genes under consideration.

Inbreeding Coefficient. — Wright's coefficient of inbreeding is a calculation of the average percentage of homozygosis to be expected from any particular system of mating The formula is

$$F_x = S[(\tfrac{1}{2})^{n+n'+1}(1 + F_a)]$$

where,

F_x is the inbreeding coefficient of the individual,

F_a is the inbreeding coefficient of the common ancestor,

n is the number of generations between the common ancestor and the sire,

n' is the number of generations between the common ancestor and the dam,

S represents summation

Mean-square Error:

$$\sqrt{\frac{S(X - \bar{x})^2}{n - 1}}$$

where X is a single observation, $\bar{x}$ the mean of all observations, S stands for summation of the series and n is the total number of observations.

Napierian Logarithms:

To convert ordinary logarithms to Napierian, multiply by 2 30259
To convert Napierian logarithms to ordinary ones, multiply by 0 43429

Phenotypes. — The maximum number of distinct phenotypes which can appear in F_2 when complete dominance obtains is given by calculating 2^n where n is the number of factors involved.

Progeny Size. — For an expected ratio of $x.y$ the probability (P) of the occurrence of at least one member of the y phenotype in a progeny of n individuals is given by ·

$$P = 1 - \frac{x^n}{(x + y)^n}$$

Progeny sizes for probability levels of 0 95, 0 99 and 0 999 are given below for simple ratios

Expected Ratio	Probability 0 95	0.99	0 999
1 1	5 plts	7 plts	10 plts
3.1	11 "	16 "	24 "
7 1	23 "	35 "	56 "
16·1	47 "	72 "	107 "
63:1	243 "	373 "	559 "

Ratios:

$$F_2 \qquad (4^n - 1):1$$
$$Backcross \quad (2^n - 1):1$$

where n is the number of factors involved.

The proportion of homozygotes to heterozygotes in a population mating at random is given by

$$p^2 : 2pq : q^2$$

where p^2 and q^2 are the proportions of the two homozygous classes respectively, $2pq$ represents the proportion of heterozygotes and $p + q = 1$. The full F_2 ratio (with dominance) is given by calculating $(3 + 1)^n$ e.g. 2 factor pairs would give $(3 + 1)^2 = 9:3:3:1$; 3 factors give $(3 + 1)^3 = 27:9:9:9:3:3:3:1$.

Recombination Fraction. — The formulae for the gametic output of the double heterozygote AaBb are (i) **Coupling:** $\frac{1}{2}(1-p)$AB, $\frac{1}{2}p$Ab, $\frac{1}{2}p$aB, $\frac{1}{2}(1-p)$ab; (ii) **Repulsion:** $\frac{1}{2}p$AB, $\frac{1}{2}(1-p)$Ab, $\frac{1}{2}(1-p)$aB, $\frac{1}{2}p$ab, where p represents the recombination fraction. Where there is no linkage, $p = 0.5$.

Relationship Coefficient. — A measure of the degree of relationship existing between any two individuals. The general formula is:

$$R_{xy} = \frac{S[(\frac{1}{2})^{n+n'}(1 + F_a)]}{\sqrt{(1 + F_x)(1 + F_y)}}$$

R_{xy} is the relationship coefficient of two individuals X and Y.

n is the number of generations X is removed from the common ancestor A.

n' is the number of generations Y is removed from the common ancestor A,

F_x is the inbreeding coefficient of X (q.v.),

F_y is the inbreeding coefficient of Y (q.v.),

F_a is the inbreeding coefficient of A.

Standard Deviation (σ):

$$\sigma = \sqrt{\frac{S(d^2)}{n - 1}}$$

where S stands for summation, d is the difference between an observation and the mean and n is the total number of observations.

Variance (σ^2). — *See* under Standard Deviation (above). The standard deviation is the square-root of the variance.

Appendix 2

Coefficients of the terms in the expansion of $(1 + x)^n$ for values of n from 1 to 20

n	Coefficients	Totals
1	1 1	2^1
2	1 2 1	2^2
3	1 3 3 1	2^3
4	1 4 6 4 1	2^4
5	1 5 10 10 5 1	2^5
6	1 6 15 20 15 6 1	2^6
7	1 7 21 35 35 21 7 1	2^7
8	1 8 28 56 70 56 28 8 1	2^8
9	1 9 36 84 126 126 84 36 9 1	2^9
10	1 10 45 120 210 252 210 120 45 10 1	2^{10}
11	1 11 55 165 330 462 462 330 165 55 11 1	2^{11}
12	1 12 66 220 495 792 924 792 495 220 66 12 1	2^{12}
13	1 13 78 286 715 1287 1716 1716 1287 715 286 78 13 1	2^{13}
14	1 14 91 364 1001 2002 3003 3432 3003 2002 1001 364 91 14 1	2^{14}
15	1 15 105 455 1365 3003 5005 6435 6435 5005 3003 1365 455 105 15 1	2^{15}
16	1 16 120 560 1820 4368 8008 11440 12870 11440 8008 4368 1820 560 120 16 1	2^{16}
17	1 17 136 680 2380 6188 12376 19448 24310 24310 19448 12376 6188 2380 680 136 17 1	2^{17}
18	1 18 153 816 3060 8568 18564 31824 43758 48620 43758 31824 18564 8568 3060 816 153 18 1	2^{18}
19	1 19 171 969 3876 11628 27132 50388 75582 92378 92378 75582 50388 27132 11628 3876 969 171 19 1	2^{19}
20	1 20 190 1140 4845 15504 38760 77520 125970 167960 184756 167960 125970 77520 38760 15504 4845 1140 190 20 1	2^{20}

2^n and 4^n for values of n from 3 to 20:

n	2^n	4^n
3	8	64
4	16	256
5	32	1,024
6	64	4,096
7	128	16,384
8	256	65,536
9	512	262,144
10	1,024	1,048,576
11	2,048	4,194,304
12	4,096	16,777,216
13	8,192	67,108,864
14	16,384	268,435,456
15	32,768	1,073,741,824
16	65,536	4,294,967,296
17	131,072	17,179,869,184
18	262,144	68,719,476,736
19	524,288	272,877,906,944
20	1,048,576	1,091,511,627,776

Appendix 4

Distribution of χ^2:

Probability

n	.99	.95	.90	.80	.70	.50	.30	.20	.10	.05	.02	.01	.001
1	0.0002	0.004	0.016	0.06	0.15	0.46	1.07	1.64	2.71	3.84	5.41	6.64	10.83
2	0.02	0.10	0.21	0.45	0.71	1.39	2.41	3.22	4.61	5.99	7.82	9.21	13.82
3	0.12	0.35	0.58	1.01	1.42	2.37	3.67	4.64	6.25	7.82	9.84	11.34	16.27
4	0.30	0.71	1.06	1.65	2.20	3.36	4.88	5.99	7.78	9.49	11.67	13.28	18.47
5	0.55	1.15	1.61	2.34	3.00	4.35	6.06	7.29	9.24	11.07	13.39	15.09	20.52
6	0.87	1.64	2.20	3.07	3.83	5.35	7.23	8.56	10.65	12.59	15.03	16.81	22.46
7	1.24	2.17	2.83	3.82	4.67	6.35	8.38	9.80	12.02	14.07	16.62	18.48	24.32
8	1.65	2.73	3.49	4.59	5.53	7.34	9.52	11.03	13.36	15.51	18.17	20.09	26.13
9	2.09	3.33	4.17	5.38	6.39	8.34	10.66	12.24	14.68	16.92	19.68	21.67	27.88
10	2.56	3.94	4.87	6.18	7.27	9.34	11.78	13.44	15.99	18.31	21.16	23.21	29.59
11	3.05	4.58	5.58	6.99	8.15	10.34	12.90	14.63	17.28	19.68	22.62	24.73	31.26
12	3.57	5.23	6.30	7.81	9.03	11.34	14.01	15.81	18.55	21.03	24.05	26.22	32.91
13	4.11	5.89	7.04	8.63	9.93	12.34	15.12	16.99	19.81	22.36	25.47	27.69	34.53
14	4.66	6.57	7.79	9.47	10.82	13.34	16.22	18.15	21.06	23.69	26.87	29.14	36.12
15	5.23	7.26	8.55	10.31	11.72	14.34	17.32	19.31	22.31	25.00	28.26	30.58	37.70
16	5.81	7.96	9.31	11.15	12.62	15.34	18.42	20.47	23.54	26.30	29.63	32.00	39.25
17	6.41	8.67	10.09	12.00	13.53	16.34	19.51	21.62	24.77	27.59	31.00	33.41	40.79
18	7.02	9.39	10.87	12.86	14.44	17.34	20.60	22.76	25.99	28.87	32.35	34.81	42.31
19	7.63	10.12	11.65	13.72	15.35	18.34	21.69	23.90	27.20	30.14	33.69	36.19	43.82
20	8.26	10.85	12.44	14.58	16.27	19.34	22.78	25.04	28.41	31.41	35.02	37.57	45.32
21	8.90	11.59	13.24	15.45	17.18	20.34	23.86	26.17	29.62	32.67	36.34	38.93	46.80
22	9.54	12.34	14.04	16.31	18.10	21.34	24.94	27.30	30.81	33.92	37.66	40.29	48.27
23	10.20	13.09	14.85	17.19	19.02	22.34	26.02	28.43	32.01	35.17	38.97	41.64	49.73
24	10.86	13.85	15.66	18.06	19.94	23.34	27.10	29.55	33.20	36.42	40.27	42.98	51.18
25	11.52	14.61	16.47	18.94	20.87	24.34	28.17	30.68	34.38	37.65	41.57	44.31	52.62
26	12.20	15.38	17.29	19.82	21.79	25.34	29.25	31.80	35.56	38.89	42.86	45.64	54.05
27	12.88	16.15	18.11	20.70	22.72	26.34	30.32	32.91	36.74	40.11	44.14	46.96	55.48
28	13.57	16.93	18.94	21.59	23.65	27.34	31.39	34.03	37.92	41.34	45.42	48.28	56.89
29	14.26	17.71	19.77	22.48	24.58	28.34	32.46	34.14	39.09	42.56	46.69	49.59	58.30
30	14.95	18.49	20.60	23.36	25.51	29.34	33.53	36.25	40.26	43.77	47.96	50.89	59.70

(Appendix 4 is abridged from Table IV of FISHER and YATES's Statistical Tables for Biological, Agricultural and Medical Research (Oliver & Boyd Ltd., Edinburgh), by kind permission of the author and publishers.)

Genotypes expected in backcrosses and in F₂s:

Monohybrids:

Backcross	1Aa 1aa
F₂	1AA ·2Aa :1aa

Dihybrids.

Backcross	1AaBb :1aaBb :1Aabb :1aabb
F₂	1AABB 2AaBB .1aaBB .
	2AABb 4AaBb 2aaBb :
	1AAbb 2Aabb :1aabb

With full dominance the F₂ phenotypes are
9AB ·3Ab 3aB ·1ab

Trihybrids:

Backcross	1AaBbCc ·1AaBbcc 1AabbCc
	1Aabbcc :1aaBbCc .1aaBbcc :
	1aabbCc :1aabbcc
F₂	1AABBCC 2AaBBCC 1aaBBCC .
	2AABBCc 4AaBBCc .2aaBBCc .
	1AABBcc 2AaBBcc 1aaBBcc :
	2AABbCC ·4AaBbCC 2aaBbCC .
	4AABbCc 8AaBbCc 4aaBbCc :
	2AABbcc 4AaBbcc 2aaBbcc :
	1AAbbCC :2AabbCC 1aabbCC :
	2AAbbCc 4AabbCc 2aabbCc
	1AAbbcc :2Aabbcc 1aabbcc

With full dominance the F₂ phenotypes are
27ABC 9ABc 9AbC :9aBC 3Abc .3abC 3aBc 1abc

Appendix 6

Percentage of homozygotes in each generation following a cross the whole progeny of which is continuously selfed (*assuming equal productivity of all types and independent segregation*).

No. of allelomorphic pairs of factors involved

	1	2	3	4	5	6	7	8	9	10	11	12	13	14	15	20	25	30	35	40	100
F_2	50.0	25.0	12.5	6.3	3.1	1.6	0.8	0.4	0.2	0.1	—	—	—	—	—	—	—	—	—	—	—
F_3	75.0	56.3	42.2	31.6	23.7	17.8	13.3	10.0	7.5	5.6	4.2	3.2	2.4	1.8	1.3	0.3	0.1	—	—	—	—
F_4	87.5	76.6	67.0	58.6	51.3	44.9	39.3	34.4	30.1	26.3	23.0	20.1	17.6	15.4	13.5	6.9	3.6	1.8	0.9	0.4	—
F_5	93.8	87.9	82.4	77.3	72.4	67.9	63.7	59.7	55.9	52.5	49.2	46.1	43.2	40.5	38.0	27.5	19.9	14.4	10.4	7.6	1.6
F_6	96.9	93.9	90.9	88.1	85.3	82.7	80.1	77.6	75.2	72.8	70.5	68.3	66.2	64.1	62.1	53.0	45.2	38.6	32.9	28.1	4.2
F_7	98.4	96.9	95.4	93.9	92.4	91.0	89.6	88.2	86.8	85.4	84.1	82.8	81.5	80.2	79.0	73.0	67.5	62.3	57.6	53.3	20.7
F_9	99.6	99.2	98.8	98.5	98.1	97.7	97.3	96.9	96.5	96.2	95.8	95.4	95.0	94.7	94.3	92.5	90.7	88.9	87.2	85.5	67.6
F_{11}	99.9	99.8	99.7	99.6	99.5	99.4	99.3	99.2	99.1	99.0	98.9	98.8	98.7	98.7	98.6	98.1	97.6	97.1	96.7	96.2	90.8
F_{13}	—	—	99.9	99.9	99.9	99.9	99.8	99.8	99.8	99.8	99.7	99.7	99.7	99.7	99.7	99.6	99.4	99.3	99.2	99.1	97.8

Numbers outside the scope of the above table can be calculated from the general formula:

$$100 \times \left(1 - \frac{1}{2^n}\right)^x$$

Where n is the number of segregating generations following a cross and x represents the number of independent allelomorphic pairs of factors involved in the cross. (The number of segregating generations is the F number minus one, e.g. F_6 represents five segregating generations.)

Rate of elimination of donor genotype by backcrossing
(neglecting the effects of selection and linkage)

		DONOR PARENT %	BACKCROSS PARENT %
F_1		50 0	50 0
1st	b-c	25 0	75 0
2nd	b-c	12 5	87 5
3rd	b-c	6 3	93 7
4th	b-c	3 1	96.9
5th	b-c	1 6	98 4
6th.	b-c	0 8	99 2
7th	b-c	0 4	99 6
8th	b-c	0 2	99 8
9th	b-c	0 1	99 9
10th	b-c	0 05	99 95

International Rules for
Symbolizing Genes and Chromosome Aberrations:

At the International Congress of Genetics held at Ithaca (N Y) in 1932, it was resolved that the genetical societies of all countries should cooperate to prepare recommendations regarding the problem of standardizing genetical symbolism in order to discuss them at the next International Genetical Congress The International Committee of Genetical Congresses appointed Professor Dr TINE TAMMES (Groningen University) to take charge of the work to be done on behalf of this resolution; in cooperation with Dr H DE HAAN, Miss TAMMES prepared a preliminary report on symbolism. Afterwards Miss TAMMES delegated the International Union of Biological Sciences to continue her task, in cooperation with the International Institute of Intellectual Cooperation at Paris, the Union convoked a meeting of delegates from various countries, which meeting was held in London in the hospitable home of the Linnean Society on August 14th and 15th, 1939 This meeting, under the presidency of Prof Dr M J. SIRKS (Groningen) was attended by the following delegates, Dr A ESTABLIER and Miss N NICOLSKY (from the I I I C. at Paris), Prof Dr O. WINGE (Denmark), Dr. B EPHRUSSI (France), Prof Dr H. NACHTSHEIM (Germany), Prof. Dr. R R GATES, Prof Dr J. B. S HALDANE and Dr. A E. WATKINS (Great Britain), Prof. Dr. K V. KOROSY (Hungary), Dr K RAMIAH and Dr. S N VENKATRAMAN (India), Prof Dr M J SIRKS and Dr S J WELLENSIEK (Netherlands), Prof. Dr O L MOHR (Norway), Miss Prof. Dr. M SKALINSKA (Poland), Dr. O. TEDIN (Sweden), Prof. Dr. F BALTZER, Prof Dr E HADORN and Prof Dr. A. ERNST (Switzerland), and Prof Dr. E W LINDSTROM (U S A) The delegates from Belgium, Italy, Finland and Japan were unable to attend.

The following rules for symbolizing genes and chromosome aberrations were drawn up

Choice of a standard type. — If it is desired to establish a standard type, this should be the most common form, as a wild type, or if such cannot be determined, the first studied most dominant form, wild or cultivated

Symbols for genes of standard type. — Generally $+$, for definite genes preferably the gene symbol with $+$ as a superscript.

Symbols for other genes. — The smallest possible number of the initial letters of the name for the character for which latin is recommended when possible

Indicating dominant and recessive. — Dominant capital initial letter, recessive small letter.

Multiple alleles. — The symbol of the first discovered allele, in small letters if recessive to standard type, with a capital initial letter if dominant to it. The standard type is designated by the same symbol with $+$ as superscript; the others by the same symbol with a special superscript in capitals for dominant, in small letters if recessive as compared to the first allele

Polymeric (multiple) genes. — Genes which cannot be distinguished by the effects and for which the loci are not known, are symbolized by the same symbol with different Arabic figures as subscript A_1, A_2, A_3, or by the same symbol with the Roman figure of the chromosome as subscript A_I, A_{II}, A_{III}

Lethal genes are indicated by the greek letter Lambda (λ) which should be reserved for them, eventually as a subscript to another symbol, or separate combined with an Arabian figure with a Roman figure for the number of the chromosome, both as a subscript (λ_1, λ_2, λ_{3IV}, etc).

Genes in polyploids. — When the chromosomes form polyvalents or if they pair at random, or if the segregation follows autopolyploid ratios, then the genes are written as many times as they are present, AAAa, AAaa, Aaaa, etc.

Groups of linked genes. — The genes written in order from left to right in the chromosome and the symbols spaced II A b c D; between those of different chromosomes a semicolon (;)

Genes in related species — The same symbol but with a subscript of the abbreviaton of the specific name.

Formulae. — Generally AABbCc, but if parental gametic genotypes are known ABc/AbC and if a linkage group is concerned and the loci of the different genes are known $\frac{a\ b\ c}{d\ e}$, the female gametic genotypes being mentioned first.

Reciprocal crosses. — In case plasmatic inheritance is involved an abbreviation of the name of the mother in parenthesis before the genotypic formula.

Priority shall be valid if no essential objection to the symbol can be made

Lettertypes. — Italics for symbols of genes, roman letters for chromosome aberrations and rearrangements.

Distances Recommended to Avoid Seed Contamination

Parts printed in Italics represent experimental results, remainder, generally practised recommendations

Crop	Isolation distance (in yards)	Authority	Year	Remarks
Brassica spp, in general	1760	Nat Inst Agric Bot [5]	1942	
	3520	Haskell[6]	1944	
Cauliflower	440	Haskell[6]	1944	
Cabbages and kale	1760	Haskell[6]	1944	
Turnip	*26*	*Tedin*[7]	*1931*	*Beyond this distance contamination remained 1%*
	880	Haskell[6]	1944	Customary in England
Radish	220	Haskell[6]	1944	
	27	*Crane and Mather*[8]	*1943*	
Beets, etc	500	Haskell[6]	1944	
	1000	Haskell[9]	1943	
Spinach	440	Haskell[6]	1944	
Carrot	880	Haskell[6]	1944	
Cucumber	220	Haskell[6]	1944	
Cotton	*1100*	*Naghibin and Uzembaev*[2]	*1934*	*'Complete'*
	16	*Naghibin and Uzembaev*[2]	*1934*	*'Practically satisfactory'*
Tomato	*55*	*Nicolaisen*[10]	*1942*	
	8	*Currence and Jenkins*[11]	*1942*	
Pea	220	Haskell[6]	1944	'Complete'
Beans (runner beans)	*330*	*Nicolaisen*[10]	*1942*	
Beans (runner and dwarf)	nil	Haskell[6]	1944	Except in stock seed
Onion	250	Haskell[6]	1944	Commercial seed
	880	Haskell[9]	1943	In Canada
	1760	Haskell[6]	1944	Stock seed
Leek	250	Haskell[6]	1944	
Sorghum	*130*	*Hsu*[12]	*1934*	
Maize	1760	Haskell[9]	1943	In Canada
	660	Salamov[13]	1940	U.S.S R Regulation before 1940
	220-330	*Salamov*[13]	*1940*	*Salamov's recommendation*
	220	Hayes and Immer[14]	1942	Minnesota Crop Improvement Association regulations
	17	*Meijers*[15]	*1937*	At this distance contamination 1 in 4,000

References:

[3]NAGHIBIN, Y., and UZEMBAEV, E., Bull. Cent. Asia. Sci. Res. Inst. Tashkent, 2 (1934).

[5]N.I.A.B., Agriculture, 49 (1942).

[6]HASKELL, G., North-Western Naturalist (1944).

[7]TEDIN, O., Landtmannen, 14 (1931).

[8]CRANE, M. B. and MATHER, K., Ann. App. Biol., 30 (1943).

[9]HASKELL, G., Nature, 152 (1943).

[10]NICOLAISEN, N., Forschungsdienst, 13 (1942).

[11]CURRENCE, T. M. and JENKINS, J. M., Proc. Amer. Soc. Hort. Sci., 41 (1942)

[12]HSU, T. S., Bull. Coll. Agric. For., Nanking, No. 25 (1934).

[13]SALAMOV, A. B., Sel. i Sem., 3 (1940).

[14]HAYES, H. K. and IMMER, F. R., "Methods of Plant Breeding" (McGraw-Hill, 1942).

[15]MEIJERS, P. G., Landbouwk Tijdschr., Wageningen, 49 (1937).

Reprinted from "Genetical Aspects of Seed-Growing" by A. J. BATEMAN in "Nature" June 8, 1946, Vol. 157, No. 3997, p. 752 by kind permission of the author and editors.

BIBLIOGRAPHY

The following publications were used in compiling this dictionary:

AGOL, I I 1931 Genetics 16.

ALTENBURG, E. 1945. Genetics (Henry Holt, New York)

ANDERSON, E & ERICKSON, R O 1941· Proc. Nat Acad. Sci Wash 27. 436-40.

ARBER, A. 1919. Amer J Sci. 48 27

BABCOCK, E. B. & CLAUSEN, R E 1927 Genetics in Relation to Agriculture (McGraw-Hill, London)

BACHARACH, A. L. & DRUMMOND, J. C. (Eds.) 1939: Vitamin E (W. Heffer & Sons, Cambridge)

BAUR, E, FISCHER, E., & LENZ, F 1931. Human Heredity. Translated by E. & C PAUL (Allen & Unwin, London)

BEADNELL, C. M 1938· Dictionary of Scientific Terms (Watts, London).

BEAL, J M 1942: Am Nat 76· 239-252

BERG, L S. 1926. Nomogenesis or Evolution determined by Law (Constable, London)

BLACKER, C. P. (Editor) 1934. The Chances of Morbid Inheritance (H K Lewis, London)

BLAKESLEE, A. F. 1944 Amer. J Bot. 31 8, p, 1s

BOURNE, G (Editor) 1945: Cytology and Cell Physiology (Oxford, Clarendon Press).

BOWER, F. O. 1939. Botany of the Living Plant (Macmillan, London)

CAIN, S. A. 1944 Foundations of Plant Geography (Harper, New York and London)

CAMP, W. H & GILLY, C. L. 1942: Brittonia 4: 323-85

CARPENTER, J. R 1938· An Ecological Glossary (Kegan Paul, Trench, Trubner and Co, London)

CHAMBER'S Technical Dictionary 1940 (W & R Chambers, London).

CHITTENDEN, R J. 1927. Vegetative Segregation (Biblio. Genetica III 355-439)

COULTER, J M. 1914: The Evolution of Sex in Plants (Univ. Chicago Press, Chicago)

CRANE, M B & LAWRENCE, W. J C. 1934: The Genetics of Garden Plants (Macmillan, London).

CREW, F. A. E. 1925. Animal Genetics (Oliver & Boyd, London).

—— 1932: Sex (In "An Outline of Modern Knowledge" edited by W. ROSE; Gollancz, London)

—— 1933: Sex Determination (Methuen, London).

CUNNINGHAM, J. T. 1921: Hormones and Heredity (Constable, London)

DARLINGTON, C D 1937· Recent Advances in Cytology (J & A. Churchill, London)
—— 1932 Chromosomes and Plant Breeding (Macmillan, London).
—— 1944 Nature (154. 164-169)
DE BEER, G R 1930. Embryology and Evolution (Clarendon Press, Oxford)
—— 1940. in The New Systematics (HUXLEY, J editor, Oxford University Press)
—— (Ed) 1938 Evolution (Clarendon Press, Oxford)
DOBZHANSKY, T. 1941 Genetics and the Origin of Species (Columbia Univ Press, New York)
DODGE, B. O 1945 Mycologia 37 629-35
DUBININ, N P. 1932: J Genet 25
EPLING, C. 1944: Science 98. 515-16
FABERGÉ, A. C 1942· Homologous Chromosomes Pairing the Physical Problem (J Genet 43 121-144)
FAGERLIND, F 1944: Hereditas 30· 590-96
FISCHER, A 1925: Tissue Culture (London)
FISHER, R A & YATES, F 1938: Statistical Tables for Biological, Agricultural and Medical Research (Oliver and Boyd, London).
FORD, E B 1940 Mendelism and Evolution (Methuen, London)
—— 1942· Genetics for Medical Students (Methuen, London)
—— 1945 Butterflies (Collins, London)
FROLOVA, S L. 1944 J Heredity 35· 235-246
GAGER, C. S 1920· Heredity and Evolution in Plants (P Blakiston's, Philadelphia).
GAVAUDAN, P 1943 C R Soc Biol Paris 137 281-83
GILMOUR, J S L. & GREGOR, J W. 1939 Nature 144 333
GOLDSCHMIDT, R 1938 Physiological Genetics (McGraw-Hill, New York).
GRAY, J 1931· A Text Book of Experimental Cytology (Cambridge University Press)
GREGOR, J W 1933 Ann Appl Biol 20 205-19
GRUENBERG, B C 1930: The Story of Evolution (Chapman & Hall, London)
GRUNEBERG, H. 1938 J. Genet 36 153-170
GUSTAFSSON, A 1944 Hereditas 30 145-51
HAGEDOORN, A L 1946 Animal Breeding (Crosby Lockwood, London)
HALDANE, J B S 1932 The Causes of Evolution (Longmans Green, London)
HARLAND, S C 1941· Proceedings of the Seventh International Genetical Congress, August 1939 138-9
HAYES, H. K & GARBER, R J 1927 Breeding Crop Plants (McGraw Hill, New York & London)
HAYES, H K & IMMER, F R 1942 Methods of Plant Breeding (McGraw-Hill, New York & London)
HENDERSON, J F & W D. 1939 A Dictionary of Scientific Terms (Oliver & Boyd, London).
HERBERT, S. 1922 The First Principles of Evolution (A & C Black, London)
HOGBEN, L 1939: Nature and Nurture (Allen & Unwin, London).
HURST, C C 1933. The Mechanism of Creative Evolution (University Press, Cambridge)

HUSKINS, C. L. 1941 Am. Nat 75 329-344

HUXLEY, J S. 1938 *In* Evolution (edited by G R DF BEER, Oxford)

—— 1938· Am Nat *72*: 416-433

HUXLEY, J. (*Ed.*) 1940 The New Systematics (Oxford University Press)

—— 1940 The Uniqueness of Man (Chatto & Windus, London).

—— 1944 Evolution. The Modern Synthesis (Allen and Unwin, London).

HUXLEY, NEEDHAM, & LERNER 1941 Nature 148. 225

Imperial Bureau of Plant Breeding & Genetics, 1930-1946. Plant Breeding Abstracts, Vol 1-16.

JACKSON, B. D 1900· A Glossary of Botanic Terms (Duckworth, London)

JONES, W N 1934 Plant Chimaeras and Graft Hybrids (Methuen, London)

JONES, S. G 1939. Introduction to Floral Mechanism (Blackie, Glasgow)

KENNETH, J. H 1943. Gestation Periods (Imp Agric. Bureaux)

KLEINSCHMIDT, O 1930 The Formenkreis Theory and the Progress of the Organic World (Witherby, London)

LAWRENCE, W J C 1937 Practical Plant Breeding (Allen and Unwin, London)

LEA, D. E. & CATCHESIDE, D G 1942 J. Genet 44 216-245.

LEVAN, A 1946· Hereditas 32· 458

LEWIS 1920. J Exp Med 31 275

LEWIS, D 1943 Physiology of Incompatibility in Plants III (J Genet. 45. 171-185).

LINDEGREN, C C. 1946 Proc Nation Acad Sci, U S. A. 32,3. 68-70.

LOCK, R H. 1920 Variation, Heredity and Evolution (John Murray, London)

LOTSY, J. P 1931 Genetica 13 1-16.

LUDFORD, R. J. 1945· *in* Cytology and Cell Physiology (edited by G. BOURNE; Oxford, Clarendon Press).

LUSH, J L 1943 Animal Breeding Plans (Iowa State College Press, Ames)

MAGUINNESS, O. D. 1940 Environment and Heredity (Nelson, London).

MATHER, K 1938· The Measurement of Linkage in Heredity (Methuen, London)

—— 1940 The Determination of Position in Crossing over (J Genet. 39· 205-223)

—— 1943· Nature 151 68

MAYR, E 1942 Systematics and the Origin of Species (Columbia Univ. Press, New York)

MENSINKAI, S W. 1939: Cytogenetic Studies in the Genus Allium (J Genet. 39: 1-45).

METZ, C W. 1938: Am Nat 72. 485-520

MEYER, H. 1938: J. Genet. 36. 329-66

MOORE, E. M 1934· Heredity, mainly Human (Chapman & Hall, London)

MORGAN, T. H. 1919: The Physical Basis of Heredity (Lippincott, Philadelphia and London)

—— 1926 The Theory of the Gene (Yale University Press, New Haven, Conn)

Morgan, T. H, Bridges, C. B & Sturtevant, A H 1925: The Genetics of Drosophila (Biblio Genetica II · 1-262)

Morgan, Sturtfvant, Muller & Bridges 1926. The Mechanism of Mendelian Heredity (Henry Holt, New York).

Mottram, V. H. 1944 The Physical Basis of Personality (Pelican)

Mottram, V. H & Graham, G 1940 · Hutchinson's Food and The Principles of Dietetics. 9th edn

Nath, Prof V, 1944. Reported in Nature 153 · 553.

Nebel, B R 1939: Botan. Review 5 563

Needham, J 1938: Biol Rev. 13. 225

Newcombe, H B. 1942. The Action of X-rays on the Cell (J. Genet. 43. 145-171).

Östergren, G & Prakken, R. 1946 Hereditas 32: 473-494

Overbfdk, J van, 1945 Science 102 621

Pincher, C. 1946 The Breeding of Farm Animals (Penguin Handbook).

Pontecorvo, G 1943 Viability Interactions Between Chromosomes (J Genet 45 51-66).

Punnett, R C 1927 · Mendelism (Macmillan, London).

Ramusson, J. 1933 Hereditas 18 245-61

Ricf, V A 1942 Breeding and Improvement of Farm Animals (McGraw-Hill, New York & London)

Robbins, W W 1924. Botany of Crop Plants (P. Blackiston's, Philadelphia).

Robson, J M 1940: Recent Advances in Sex and Reproductive Physiology (J & A Churchill, London).

Sansome, E 1945 Nature 156 47.

Sansome, F W & Philp, J 1939 Recent Advances in Plant Genetics (J & A Churchill, London)

Schopffr, W H 1943 Plants and Vitamins (Chronica Botanica, Waltham, Mass)

Sharp, L W 1943 Fundamentals of Cytology (McGraw-Hill, New York & London)

Shull, A F 1938 Heredity (McGraw-Hill, New York).

Sinnott, E W & Dunn, L C. 1939: Principles of Genetics (McGraw-Hill, New York).

Southwick, W. E 1939 · Am Nat 73 44-68

Sprague, G. F. & Tatum, L. A 1942: J Amer Soc Agron 34 · 923-32

Stephens, S G 1942 Colchicine Produced Polyploids in Gossypium, I (J Genet 44 272-295).

Sturtevant, A H & Beadle, G W. 1940. An Introduction to Genetics (W B Saunders, Philadelphia & London).

The Journal of Heredity 1937, 28 2

Thomas, P. T 1940: J Genet 40 119-128, p. 123.

Thompson, D H 1931. Genetics 16.

—— 1938. Am. Nat 72: 53-58.

Thorpe, W. H. 1930. Biol. Rev 5 · 177

Timofeeff-Ressovsky, N W 1940 In The New Systematics (Huxley, J, editor; Oxford University Press).

Tobgy, H. A 1943. J Genet. 45 67-111.

Turesson, G 1922 · Hereditas 3 · 211

Vitamin B₂ Complex, The, 1945 Nature 156 · 86-7.

Waddington, C. H. 1939: An Introduction to Modern Genetics (Allen & Unwin, London).

—— 1942: Nature 150: 563.

—— 1942: The Epigenotype (Endeavour 1, 1: 18-20).

Walter, H. E. 1940: Genetics. An Introduction to the Study of Heredity (Macmillan, New York).

White, M. J. D. 1937: The Chromosomes (Methuen, London).

Wigan, L. G. 1944: J. Genet. 46: 140-60.

Wilson, E. B. 1925: The Cell in Development and Heredity (Macmillan, New York).

Willis, J. C. 1922: Age and Area (Cambridge University Press).

Winters, L. M. 1944: Animal Breeding (Wiley, New York; Chapman and Hall, London).

Wright, Sewall, 1946: Genetics 31: 39.

Yearbook of Agriculture, U. S. Dept. Agric. 1936.

Lightning Source UK Ltd.
Milton Keynes UK
UKOW04f0006111216

289652UK00022B/882/P